Collecting Baseball, Basketball, Football and Hockey Cards

Collecting Baseball, Basketball, Football and Hockey Cards

Paul Green and Tony Galovich

Bonus Books, Inc., Chicago

97 96 95 94 93   5 4 3 2 1

Library of Congress Catalog Card Number: 92-74147

International Standard Book Number: 0-929387-84-8

Bonus Books, Inc.
160 East Illinois Street
Chicago, Illinois 60611

Printed in the United States of America

Contents

Acknowledgments

M any people play a behind-the-scenes role in a book. Always there is family, which in this case especially means Emily and Andrew Green. Kathy and Kit also deserve special recognition for their constant roles in encouraging my various projects.

Greg Behrendt of Behrendt Photography made a valuable contribution in the form of all the pictures for this effort. Hal Hintze chipped in with a superb job on the chapter on modern cards.

Key West has been a special place for many writers. Perhaps it's the atmosphere, the attitude or the unique blend of people who inhabit the end of the road. I tend to think it's the latter, and want to recognize some of them who make a difference to me.

It's doubtful that any bar in America has the history of literary achievement represented by the patrons of Capt. Tony's in Key West. As the original watering hole for Ernest Hemingway and virtually who has visited or stayed in Key West since, the people of Capt. Tony's have to be mentioned. They include Joey and Nancy Faber, Suzanne and Doug

Leps, eternal Braves fan Lori, Karen and a host of "regulars" who know who they are.

Down the street at the Pier House Beach club, lively sports enthusiasts John and Joan (who has somehow proven that the Enlish theater and American sports can mix) deserve mention.

A few others in Key West must also be mentioned. Kenny Lavoie started as a landlord and has become a friend. Amy Kamil Brown at Inter Arts has proven ther is life after Capt. Tony's. Tom Walker, on of Key West's finest, is also one of Key West's best unrecognized writers. Moreover, as all the locals know, he's a significant moderating factor when my worst instincts appear. Others such as my male bonding buddy Bill, Laurie, Lucia and Coral keep life at the end of the road lively.

An assortment of others around the country should be noted. Diane, Sam, Charlie, Brian, Reed and others too numerous to mention have had a hand in one way or another in creating this book.

Lastly, I need to thank co-author Tony Galovich. Tony has always been ahead of his time in recognizing cards for their investment potential and risks. Whether it's his newsletter, his columns or now this book, when someone has had something interesting to say about investing in cards, that someone has frequently been Tony.

P.G.

Introduction

It used to be simple. You bought cards as a kid, played with them, traded them and eventually left them as your interests changed. Those were the 1950s and 1960s. All that changed in the early 1980s when a slightly odd band of characters tried to recapture their youth by beginning their card collections again. Most laughed, but these people started making money and the laughing stopped.

Today, the early 1980s seem like another era and not just another decade. Topps, Fleer and Donruss baseball cards have turned into dozens of companies and at least four major sports with a host of others in waiting. What used to be simple is now a complex market where millions of dollars are made and lost routinely. Experts and the nation's financial and sporting press now follow the ups and downs of prices for cards and related sports material as they follow IBM or the NFL Central Division race.

In this atmosphere the novice and often even the experienced collector need all the help and information they can find. Sadly, it's often very little, as so far the growth in information about cards has not kept pace with the size of the market for them.

We set out to cover the cards of four sports from their inception in the late 1880s to the present day. It was too large a task. As most start with the cards of today or the cards of their youth, it made sense to complete work on this portion of the card market first. Without a doubt, cards from 1948 to the present day represent the overwhelming percentage of sales in the current card market.

Our decision to cover the four major sports was an easy one. You need only look at today's market and you will discover that there is an active market in football, basketball and hockey cards as well as baseball. In some respects it's a little frightening. Millions of cards, millions of dollars and little hard information in book form on baseball cards and virtually nothing save price guides on the other three sports.

We have plunged into that information void with modest expectations. There is much to be learned about both the cards and the card market. We hope others will add to what we've done, but at least for the present what follows is a start toward a better understanding of modern cards.

Middle-Period Cards 1948-1980

You can call cards made between 1948 and 1980 "middle-period" cards. They have all the advantages of the cards that came before them, but none of the disadvantages. Or maybe the other way around. The sets are more regular and systematic, but there's less virgin territory to explore. You'll find more of them out there than cards from before World War II, but often at higher prices. The trouble is that people get all emotional over them. Cards from this era bring back memories, powerful memories; they were out in enough numbers that practically everyone around the country could have found a store somewhere nearby where they could have bought a pack or two, and held onto them for a time until they went off to school or discovered girls or whatever and the cards were thrown out. Or maybe they weren't thrown out, and mouldered in a shoebox in an attic for years until they were discovered, and the discoverer got all misty-eyed over what they were and what they meant to him, good times with Tommy Mahoney and Seymour Irschenbaum at P.S. 27, and jujubes and Saturday double-features at the Oriental

Theatre and *Howdy Doody* and all that squishy nostalgia stuff. Do they want to part with their childhood stash? Not for all the money in the world. And so we wind up talking about irrationality in what ought to be a rational market.

Somehow you have to transcend this mush when you buy middle-period cards. You have to resist the temptation to spend $500 for a Duke Snider card just because you can remember your dad taking you to Ebbets Field to see him play, and buying you popcorn and a pennant, and carrying you out of the stands when you fell asleep. Ebbets Field is torn down now; the memories are just that, nothing more. If you think they are something more, you'd better not be buying cards of these people and expecting to make money on them. You cannot balance sensible card buying and your own memories. If you want to indulge your feelings of nostalgia by buying some cards, fine. (Buy a low-grade card; it's safer.) But don't also be thinking that those cards you buy are better than Triple-A municipal bonds, too. You can't have it both ways.

However, nothing says you can't profit when other people want to indulge their nostalgia. There is much more demand for middle-period cards than there is supply. Some of this demand is latent; that is, people want the cards but don't know they want the cards until they see the cards. A lot of mid-grade cards of the 1950s and 1960s Hall of Famers are impulse buys: A fellow walks through the aisles at a card show, sees a VG-EX Sandy Koufax card, says, "Oooh, I've gotta have it," and plunks down $45 for it, practically sight-unseen. Once he gets it home, he doesn't know what he's going to do with it, or what possessed him to pay that much for it, but he's got it. His memories are indulged at a reasonable price, and a dealer sells a card that conventional wisdom would have you believe is unsaleable.

No card is unsaleable. Cards are just priced out of line with the market, and people's perception of what the market is and what these cards ought to be worth. Football, baseball and hockey cards of Hall of Famers from the '50s and '60s are expensive. No one argues with the fact that these cards ought to be expensive. But when it comes down to reality, dollars and cents, card buyers blanch at $300 for a 1953 Bowman black-and-white Casey Stengel or a $225 1961-62 Topps Bobby Hull, regardless if that's the going rate based on what the market is bearing. It's this sort of perception that keeps people out of the market, not necessarily the fact of the $300 for Stengel or the $225 for Hull. Most people can afford to shell out $300 for something. It's just the notion of $300 for a baseball card of Casey Stengel that gives many prospective card buyers pause.

If that describes you, what you have to do then is find cards from this era that provide value—or at least the perception of value. That means cards of '50s Hall of Famers that are valued at less than cards of other '50s Hall of Famers for no apparent, significant or enduring reason; cards of '60s Hall of Famers that are valued at less than cards of other '60s Hall of Famers for no compelling reason, and a few cards of possible '60s Hall of Famers; and cards of some selected '70s Hall of Famers and Hall of Fame probables.

Each decade has its own collecting strategy. As far as the '50s go, just about anyone who's going to be enshrined out of the decade has been enshrined. The notion that Richie Ashburn belongs in the Hall of Fame has some merit, and you can argue for Ashburn until you're blue in the face, but it really, truly appears as though Ashburn will not make it, and so neither will his cards. The same holds for Lionel Taylor in football. The jury has spoken, and the verdict is thumbs down. And face it: Hall of Famers are the only cards from this era that sell consistently well.

What about sets? Prices for commons tend to lag far behind the prices for sets, and even farther behind the prices for stars, and those gaps are widening. What that means is that the demand for commons, the real stuff a set is made of, is slackening. Fewer people are completing sets. Fewer people want sets. Fewer people can afford sets. More people want what they consider to be the stuff of a set: cards of individual stars. If you want to buy and sell cards as sets, more power to you. You're showing off your stripes as a true collector. But you'd better steel yourself for some lonely days ahead.

Any sort of card investment is a speculation. What you're speculating on when you buy cards of '50s and '60s players are irregularities in the pricing of cards within a given set, series or run of sets. It's not until you start buying cards of '70s players that you can allow yourself the relative luxury of speculating on the ability of players to attain lasting fame.

THE 1950s

BASEBALL

Cards of the '50s in particular are a very technical investment, because the area has been picked over so much by so many card buyers. It's strange, but the era where cards invoke the most nostalgia is also the era where card buying is most technical.

Given those constraints, '50s baseball would seem to be the toughest buy of all. And it is. Baseball cards from the '50s are richest in nostalgia of all cards. The glory of old Bowmans and Topps' very first cards has been celebrated in books *(The Great American Baseball Card Flipping, Trading and Bubblegum Book)* and passed from collector to collector. The game was arguably better then than it ever had been or ever will be. Even the scrubs were good, and if they weren't good at least they were well-remembered.

You can't underestimate the importance, historical and otherwise, of Topps and Bowman. Bowman, along with Leaf, was the first company to bring back sports cards to postwar candy counters. Bowman was the corporate successor to Gum, Inc., makers of the Play Ball series of the late '30s and early '40s, and a powerful force in the gum-and-candy business, especially in the Northeast. Its cards mixed occasionally lovely art with offhanded charm; they often kept the same style across sports, so that 1950 Bowman football and 1950 Bowman baseball look very much alike. Throughout the early '50s, Bowman had the edge on Topps for player selection. Bowman, not Topps, had the first cards of Mickey Mantle, Stan Musial and Willie Mays, and the first postwar cards of Ted Williams. And Mantle and Mays are as good a place as any to start picking cards.

In 1951 Bowman made cards of two young ballplayers, Mickey Mantle (#253) and Willie Mays (#305). The next year Topps included cards of the same ballplayers in its inaugural series. The Bowman cards were in that set's scarcest number series; the Mantle from the next year's Topps set would be as well. Print runs for the two sets are roughly equivalent; we don't have any way of knowing the exact numbers for each. The scarcest number series of 1952 Topps cards is scarcer than the scarcest number series of

'51 Bowmans, but everything else is essentially a wash. You can't explain away the differences in value between the '51 Bowmans and '52 Topps on any cards except those in that highest '52 Topps number series.

Anyway, to return to our story. The true rookie cards, supposedly the most significant and valuable cards of any player, of Mickey Mantle and Willie Mays are in the 1951 Bowman set, and they're expensive. The Mantle brings $5,000 and the Mays $2,500. But while they're expensive, they're also undervalued.

How can that be? Simple. If you accept the fact that a player's most valuable card ought to be his rookie card, then the '51 Bowmans of Mantle and Mays ought to be most valuable on principle alone. And if you also accept the fact that Mantle and Mays were the most dominant players of the greatest decade of baseball in history—forgive us, Teddy Ballgame—then these cards ought to be the two most valuable cards of the postwar era, rarities notwithstanding.

And they're not.

Heck, they're not even close. A 1953 Topps Mickey Mantle—the Mick's third-year card, for crying out loud—is as much as a Willie Mays rookie. Same with a '52 Topps Eddie Mathews. And a 1952 Topps Mickey Mantle—well, a 1952 Topps Mickey Mantle is *10 times* the price of a '51 Bowman of Willie Mays.

Is that right? Is that fair? Of course not. It only makes sense if you ascribe totally to the '52 Topps mystique.

The 1952 Topps set is the jewel in the crown, the standard by which all others are judged. Puppies bark for it. It's not the first set ever produced by Topps, and it does not have the rookie cards of Mantle and Mays. And people love it, beyond all reason.

The reasons why people love it start with its size. It's the first big set of big cards. While it wasn't the first baseball set Topps ever did (its 1951 Red Backs and Blue Backs have that honor), it was the first major set made by Topps, and the first set where series were a major factor in card distribution and worth. It's considered, rightly or wrongly, to be the first set of the modern era. It's also an uncommonly good-looking set, except for that card of Gus Zernial with six baseballs nailed to a bat that, if it had been a play, would have been written by Samuel Beckett.

But those reasons are hardly adequate to explain the prices the set brings. The entire set catalogs for $60,000, with the aforementioned Mantle card accounting for $25,000 of that. The most common card from the high-number series goes for $175. Top-grade '52 Topps cards aren't actually bought and sold as much as they're looked at and talked about and syndicated. You can't approach this set with any sense of rationality and come away satisfied.

Want some advice on the '52 Topps set? Save your money. Either the set will continue to go up in value at the same rate as the sets around it—it'll become even more unaffordable, in other words—or it'll plateau and the sets around it will catch up to it. The days when the '52 Topps set could whip any other set on the block at price appreciation are gone.

Buy the '51 Bowman Mantle and Mays cards if you're looking to spend big bucks out of the early '50s. Not only are these cards undervalued by comparison, but indications are that increasing numbers of people are seeing them as being undervalued. And what good are undervalued cards if no one else but you considers them to be undervalued?

Here's a good example. I once wrote about the 1952 Topps Willie Mays and remarked what a good buy it was at $1,500. I checked the price two weeks later and the card was $1,800. Other people realized what I had: That the 1952 Topps Mays is an undervalued card. And it really is; $1,800 for this card is relatively reasonable. Relatively reasonable: People outside of the sportscard hobby are going to think you're nuts for spending $1,800 for a single piece of 40-year-old cardboard, even if it is a very attractive piece of 40-year-old cardboard with the picture of the best all-around player of the '50s on it. But when you add up the numbers for the cards around it, there's a hole here that can only be filled by about a 20 percent increase in value.

While people focus on the 1952 Topps set, it's to the neglect of the 1952 Bowman set, which is arguably one of the top three or four baseball-card sets of the postwar era. It may lack Ted Williams but it has Stan Musial, and it's about one-third the price of a '52 Topps Mickey Mantle. If you have $8,500 sitting around—hey, and who doesn't?—and you want to spend it on something that'll bring you pleasure and will still increase in value 15 percent a year, this is the item to go for. If you haven't got that $8,500 sitting around and don't mind a couple months of tunafish and macaroni and cheese, consider the Mays ($900) and Mantle ($2,000) cards out of this set; better yet, how about Stan Musial ($500) in one of his rare card appearances? If that's still too much, how about a card or two of a second-echelon Hall of Famer? They really are affordable.

Look at it this way: You'll pay $75 or more for a 1990 Leaf Frank Thomas card. You'll pay at least that for an Upper Deck Ken Griffey, Jr., rookie or a 1986 Donruss Jose Canseco. These are all powerful cards and their possibilities are pretty strong, but compared to top-grade '50s cards of Hall of Famers they're as common as Toyotas in the suburbs. Not only do they lack the character of older cards, they lack plain old scarcity. There are hundreds of thousands of top-grade Leaf Thomas cards and millions of Upper Deck Griffey rookies; there weren't even hundreds of thousands of 1952 Bowman Warren Spahn cards made, much less kept in anything approaching collectible condition. And while Frank Thomas and Jose Canseco and Ken Griffey, Jr., may go on to have Hall of Fame careers, they're not there yet and may never get there, and Warren Spahn is. Warren Spahn is one of the two or three greatest pitchers to ever put on a uniform, yet his '52 Bowman card costs about as much as any of these three rookie cards. Maybe that's not a true statistical irregularity, but it's damned peculiar. And if you want a '52 Bowman of Hall of Famers Ralph Kiner, Early Wynn, Johnny Mize, George Kell or Enos Slaughter, you'll only have to spend $40 to $75. Rare cards. Great cards. Great players. How could they do anything but go up in value? All the variables— career stats, print runs, demographics, scarcity in grade—are all in their favor.

The 1953 sets are tough from a value standpoint, but beautiful any other way you look at them. The 1953 Bowman set is arguably the most attractive of the postwar sets, a real purist's set, and the 1953 Topps set just got a major boost when Topps reprinted it as part of its Archives series. But the Bowman color/

Bowman black-and-white combo from that year is $12,500 and the Topps set is $13,000. Not a lot of disparity there, and not a lot of value.

But who buys sets, anyway? These are sets to cherrypick for Hall of Famers and neat cards. The Hank Bauer/Yogi Berra/Mickey Mantle card in the '53 Bowman color set, for instance. It's an unusual, very attractive in-the-dugout-lazing-about shot of the three players and the first multi-player special card of the postwar era. And it's only $350. Peanuts, when you consider the Mantle card out of that same set is $1,500 and Berra alone is $500. Second-echelon Hall of Famers like Kell and Slaughter and Kiner will only run you $30 to $80 in this set, and are certainly worth all of that. Mantle and Mays are all well and good, but the passing of time will do more to bring some of these other Hall of Famers up to the level of Mantle and Mays than it will to further separate them from the pack. (That's an assumption on my part that hasn't exactly been borne out by numbers in the past. If you don't agree with it, don't buy the cards.)

The '53 Topps and Bowman sets really show a divergence in philosophy between the two big cardmakers, and a 180-degree turnaround from their previous sets. The '52 Bowman set was an art set; the cards were obviously made from paintings, which were not-so-obviously made from photographs. The '52 Topps set consisted of hand-colored, black-and-white photographs. In 1953 Bowman went the photographic route, with the first color photographs ever used on major-league cards, and Topps went the art route. In this case Bowman had the edge. But it would be the last time.

Because of the popularity of the Topps Archives '53s, regular '53 Topps are not a particularly good buy right now. If you feel you must drop $650 for Jackie Robinson or $225 for Yogi Berra, go right ahead. If you're a sucker for historical significance, Satchel Paige is all right at $450. But the affordable cards here are of guys like George Kell ($60), Hoyt Wilhelm ($70) and Ralph Kiner ($50). Get beyond those guys and you're asking for trouble.

Just so you know, the main reason the Jackie Robinson cards is $650 in this set is because it's card #1. First and last cards from middle-period sets are always quite a bit more expensive than cards from the middle of the deck because kids would keep their cards in numerical order and then stick a rubber band around them, notching the first and last cards. It doesn't help matters that Topps and Bowman would make big names like Jackie Robinson and Ted Williams their #1 cards. On the other hand, card #280 in the '53 Topps set is Milt Bolling, and he's $350. It's an interesting choice.

The '54 sets are the first ones that show a wide gap in price and perception between Topps and Bowman. The '54 Topps set has the perception of being the more desirable of the two because of the rookie cards of Hank Aaron, Al Kaline and Ernie Banks, so naturally the '54 Bowman is the one to buy. The three big rookie cards in the Topps set don't begin to explain the $4,000 gap in price between the two—and it's not like the '54 Bowman set is stripped of stars, either. Any Hall of Fame card out of that set is a good buy.

Bowman exited stage right in 1955 with a corny, TV-bordered, 320-card set. It has the only cards of some Hall of Fame umpires and second-year cards of Aaron, Kaline and Banks; if you can stand to look at them, the cards of Red Schoendienst, Early Wynn, Enos Slaughter, Pee Wee Reese, Eddie Mathews, Lou Boudreau, Ralph Kiner, and even Bob Feller aren't bad buys out of this set.

The focus shifts back to Topps for good with the 1955 and '56 sets, which are sort of the Tweedledum and Tweedledee of card sets. They look alike, they talk alike, they hate each other very much, and they're expensive—$7,000 and rising. They have loads of good cards—the rookie cards of Harmon Killebrew, Sandy Koufax and Roberto Clemente, for starters—but their price really is prohibitive. If you're going to do any shopping out of these sets, stick to the 1956 set for the second-year cards of Killebrew, Clemente and Koufax. They're much more affordable and statistically much better buys. They look swell, too. The last card of Jackie Robinson is also in this set, and it makes a nice cultural icon, if you're so inclined.

The '56 Topps set really tests your belief in certain assumed principals of card buying—like the significance of second-year cards. If you buy into the notion that if a player's rookie card is his most valuable, then his second-year card (assuming no mitigating circumstances like placement in a high-number series) ought to be second-most valuable. In real life that's usually the case, though there's no statistical agreement on what percentage of a player's rookie card his second-year card ought to be valued at. That makes buying these cards darn vexing and slightly risky. But if you want cards from the '50s you're always going to be making compromises and taking risks.

By the time you get around to the '57 Topps set, things change. Cards begin to standardize with the '57 set. Pictures are the mixture of full-color stadium shots and close-up head shots that would be Topps' stock in trade for the next twenty-five years. Set size begins to stabilize with this set, and multi-player special cards begin to appear, as Topps begins to increase the number of cards and series in order to prolong the card-selling season. Checklist cards begin to become more of a big deal with this set, too.

The most significant cards in the '57 Topps set are Frank ($250) and Brooks ($350) Robinson, but the best buys out of the set are guys like Eddie Mathews ($35) and the rookie card of Whitey Herzog ($25), which is about as interesting a buy as you can make out of this entire decade. But outside of those few cards, you're still paying $100 for a Duke Snider card in this set, a card with no particular significance. That's a stiff price for what is essentially a middle-of-the-pack card. And it's by no means out of line with the rest of the middle-of-the-pack cards in this set.

It's more of the same, really, in the 1958 set, with the exception of some of the more common white-letter variations of Hall of Famers. A white-letter Luis Aparicio is $15; a much scarcer yellow-letter variation is $50. While the yellow-letter variation is much scarcer, it's not only going to be harder to find and buy, it's going to be much harder to sell for that price when the time comes because the variation is esoteric. How many people do you think care enough about that yellow-letter variation to pay $35 more for it? Variations of this type, no matter how scarce they are and no matter how significant the card affected by the variation, just don't excite the majority of card buyers. About the only thing they really do is slightly depress the price of the more common variety, creating a buying opportunity. It all comes back to the basic equation of card buying: What stands a better chance of increasing in price by a greater percentage—a 50-cent card or a $3 card? That $15 Luis Aparicio card has a lot more headroom than a $50 Aparicio card.

By the time you get around to the '59s, Duke Snider is edging into affordability at $60 and Stan Musial's back, albeit at $150. (Musial's disappearance from cards through most of the '50s is the baseball-card equivalent of *Unsolved Mysteries;* about the only thing we know for certain is that UFOs didn't kidnap him.)

About this time multi-player special cards become more of a viable option. My opinion on multi-player special cards is this: The No. 1 card of a player is going to be his most valuable card 99 percent of the time, will go up in price before any of his other cards 99 percent of the time, will go up more 99 percent of the time and, all other things being equal, is more desirable 100 percent of the time. I cannot think of an instance in baseball cards of the '50s where, if you had a choice between an all-star card of Ernie Banks and Banks' regular card, you would want the all-star card—even taking number series into account. But if you can't afford the regular cards of a player and want some kind of card of that player you're forced to consider multi-player or special cards. That's okay; choose carefully, think of the card as a cross between a common and that player's regular card (but with loads more character), scale back your expectations 25 percent, and you should do just fine.

Actually, if you do that you'll probably wind up with cards like the "Dodgers' Boss and Power" card from the 1958 set, which features Walter Alston and Duke Snider and is quite a buy at $15, and the Aaron-Mathews "Fence Busters" card from the '59 set for $50. If you want single cards, any of the high-number all-star cards from the '59 set make good, tough buys, especially the $30 Warren Spahn all-star card (#571).

One more card from this set that deserves a mention is #338, the first and only card showing Phillies infielder George Anderson—"Sparky"—as a player. Subsequent cards showed him as a manager, and subsequent events showed him to be one of the top managers in history. He's a Hall of Famer, and $30 for his card is not too much of a price to pay. But bear in mind: It's more than doubled in the past two years.

BASKETBALL

Postwar basketball cards took a while to get rolling—like about twenty years. The National Basketball Association in those days was an amusement, like wrestling, nothing like the fights and nowhere near even football as a pro sport, and so cards showing basketball players didn't have a high likelihood of success. And to be honest, both sets from the era stiffed; what we're left with are a couple of very tough sets, and some nearly impossible cards.

Forget about putting together either a 1948-49 Bowman set ($5,100) or a 1957-58 Topps set ($3,900). You couldn't find someone to sell you the cards at that price, even if you had the money. Forget about each set's literal big man: George Mikan ($2,700) in the Bowman set and Bill Russell ($1,900) in the Topps. Go instead for the fine players in either set that are undervalued by comparison: Jumpin' Joe Fulks in the '48-'49 Bowman set ($185) and Bob Cousy in the Topps set ($275). Neither guy is going to double your money for you, but they're significant cards of great players. And the same with Dolph Schayes ($35), Cliff Hagan ($30) and Paul Arizin ($30) in the Topps set. By the standards you have to apply to these cards and sets, they're bargains. They just don't look much like conventional bargains, that's all.

FOOTBALL

Football cards of the '50s are every bit the counterpart of baseball cards when it comes to variety and style—and price. Throw out Mickey Mantle and Willie Mays and you couldn't choose between the two.

On the other hand, because there is no Mickey Mantle or Willie Mays, the most significant football cards of the best players are more affordable. It's a whole lot easier to rationalize $325 for the first card of Sammy Baugh than it is $1,500 for a Hank Aaron rookie. And Baugh is as expensive as most of the early rookies get. Okay, there's Otto Graham at $500 in the '50 Bowman set, but he's not worth that. Neither is Tom Landry ($600) in the '51 Bowman set. Not when you can pick up Sid Luckman for $150 or Bob Waterfield for $175 in either of the '48 sets.

You heard right; either of the '48 sets. Leaf was a slightly bigger player in football cards for a slightly longer time. Its '48 and '49 sets provide an interesting alternative to the Bowman sets. In fact, its 1949 set makes a decent buy for a couple of reasons: it has cheap second-year cards of some players who have more expensive first-year cards, it's the only 1949 set, and it's only $1,250. When you realize that the prices for sets tend to go up rather sharply from there, it's a good buy by comparison.

Speaking of those sets that go up rather sharply, meet the Bowman sets of the early '50s. Not that it mattered, but Bowman was not seriously challenged by Topps in football. Topps issued a felt-pennant-backed set of college football players in 1950 and a magic-less "Magic" set of collegians in 1951, but these sets are full of no-name players and aren't considered to be major sets. That doesn't mean they're bad sets; the '50 set is a tough set of tiny cards and includes the first cards of Hall of Famers Doak Walker and Ernie Stautner and the very first card of Penn State coach Joe Paterno, and the '51 set has . . . well, Vic Janowicz. But it's cheap.

The '50 Bowman set, at $3,750, is definitely not cheap. But it's cheaper than the '50 Bowman baseball set and a lot more significant, because it's the first set to incorporate the great players who came into the NFL after the demise of the All-America Football Conference. Rookie cards in the set include Y.A. Tittle, Lou Groza, Tony Canadeo, Joe Perry, Marion Motley, Otto Graham ($500? Come on!), Elroy Hirsch, and Tom Fears. The individual card buys in the bunch are Fears ($75), Motley ($65), Perry ($95), and probably the best card ever of Sammy Baugh ($115).

The next year's Bowman set features Norm Van Brocklin (eminently avoidable at $150), Tom Landry (really eminently avoidable at $600), Emlen Tunnell (good at $75) and Ernie Stautner (good at $60) and a darn nice design. There's really nothing that makes this set $3,000 (or $12,000) less significant than the two 1952 Bowman sets that came after it other than Frank Gifford's rookie card, and even that cleft chin that launched a thousand cruise ships isn't worth that kind of scratch. If you must buy a football set from the early '50s, either the '50 or the '51 is the set to buy. After that things get kind of silly.

Well, Bowman doesn't help matters any. The company issued two versions of its '52 set—small-dimensioned and more common, and large-dimensioned and scarce. The small set isn't all that common and the large set is very scarce, and there are short prints all over the place in the large set, further complicating matters. But the large cards are drop-dead gorgeous and they're full of values, despite that weighty $12,000 price tag. I'd buy large Gino Marchetti rookie cards all day at $100. Same with Paul Brown cards at $100 and George Halas cards at $150. Even Yale Lary at $125 makes quite a bit of sense. The small versions are only $25 or $30 cheaper, and in this case it makes sense to buy scarcity. The numbers are in your favor.

The '53 Bowman set is pretty but disposable. The '54 set is uglier but less disposable; there's a George Blanda rookie card in the set, a Doug Atkins rookie (recommended at $35), and a Whizzer White card in the set for $12.50 that's a darn nice buy. The '55 set throws in the rookie cards of Hall of Famers John Henry Johnson ($35), Alan Ameche ($30), Bob St. Clair ($30), Jim Ringo ($35) and Frank Gatski ($30). You could find worse ways to spend $1,350.

Topps showed up on the scene in 1955 with a set of all-time college greats that was received much better than you thought it would have been. At one time it was an absolute dog on the market but now people pursue it for the cards of Knute Rockne ($250), Red Grange ($275), Jim Thorpe ($400) and the Four Horsemen ($500). It may be the best all-time-greats set ever, but it's still an all-time-greats set, and therefore a less-than-recommended buy. It's like a bond with less than a AAA rating; you can get your money out of it and maybe even a sizable return, but it comes at the cost of doubt gnawing at the back of your skull. Your choice.

Topps took over in 1956, and the sets from there to the end of the decade are notable for the occasional big rookie (Roosevelt Brown and Lenny Moore in '56; Bart Starr, John Unitas and Paul Hornung in '57; Jim Brown and Sonny Jurgensen in '58; Bobby Mitchell and Jim Parker in 1959) and their consistently horrid designs. The biggest rookies (Brown, Hornung, Starr, Unitas) are boundlessly expensive; better to load up on second-tier Hall of Famers and second-year cards, which back off anywhere from 30 percent to 70 percent from rookie-card prices.

Football cards of the '50s follow many of the same price patterns as '50s baseball cards, only with a five-year delay. The biggest baseball cards of the decade show up in the 1951-53 sets; in football cards, they show up in the '56-'59 sets. And that delay sticks with football cards well into the '60s.

HOCKEY

Hockey cards of the '50s are the most expensive sports cards of the decade, on a year-by-year, card-by-card basis. Even the commons for any '50s set are $10 and up. The rookie cards of minor stars easily fetch $150, while the rookie cards of the game's top stars go for $500 and up. It's hard to find bargains among these cards. Maybe you shouldn't even try.

It might be fun to try to assemble a type-set collection of these cards, though, because there really were some interesting hockey cards issued during the decade. Most of the issuing was done by Parkhurst, an idiosyncratic Canadian company that thought nothing of using the same design for three or four years running or devoting the entire back of a card to an awful cartoon that made Bazooka Joe look like Krazy Kat. Parkhurst's first sets are exceptionally ugly, and that's exacerbated by the fact that many of the game's most legendary players make their appearances in these sets. So if you want a Gordie Howe rookie card, you not only have to pay $2,500 for it, but you get a tiny, rough-cut, awkwardly hand-tinted, blank-backed card in return. Is it a good deal? Well, people have paid more for stamps that looked worse. But that didn't make them sane, either.

Through the latter half of the decade Topps and Parkhurst divided the National Hockey League in two; as a result, Toronto and Montreal players were shown on Parkhurst cards, while Topps issued cards of players from American teams. It means you can't get Jacques Plante and Gordie Howe in the same set, but it also means if you don't like Andy Bathgate you don't have to buy a set that has Andy Bathgate in it. This time the disadvantages outweigh the advantages.

It's very difficult to recommend any hockey cards or sets from this period. The cards have always been collected intensely, and demand has almost always exceeded supply; as a result, there are no statistical black holes to exploit. Everything is priced to a level, and few cards move within a set unless the whole set moves. This is one case where you get what you pay for; nothing more, nothing less.

The Simple Sixties and Seventies

T he '60 and '70s seem like a simple time, baseball-card wise—and they are. They're a time of innocence, of confidences. Long ago, it must be, I have a photograph...see what I mean? Start talking about '60s baseball cards and you're as likely to wind up quoting Simon and Garfunkel songs or reminiscing about *Gilligan's Island* as you are to make any headway on the intended subject.

But the '60s really were a simple time. Bowman was dead. Fleer and Leaf, except for a couple of efforts that were over almost before they begun, were non-factors. Score and Upper Deck were just gleams in their daddies' eyes. Antitrust suits were nowhere to be found. Cards were issued in series, packs were cheap, gum was big, the same stable of players played through most of the decade, and the whole thing motored along so smoothly it's sickening.

THE 1960s AND 1970s

BASEBALL

Ten Topps sets. That's really all there is to baseball cards through the '60s. There are a couple of interesting subsets, some bonus items, a few scattered items from other manufacturers, and ten Topps sets. Where's the fun in that?

Okay, there's some fun to be had in '60s cards, but it's awfully compartmentalized. Just like the '50s, the '60s and '70s are well-documented history that have become hard-to-shake nostalgia. There are the stars and the everybody elses, and time is not likely to turn many of those everybody elses into stars, so you're forced to cherry-pick high-number and second-year cards of Hall of Famers, and perhaps take the occasional flyer on a could-be Hall of Famer.

The first thing you do with '60s cards is stay away from the obvious. Avoid the Pete Rose rookie card. Avoid the Reggie Jackson rookie card. Stay away from the Nolan Ryan rookie card like the plague. These cards are like tours of Britain. What are you possibly going to see or find out that hasn't been seen or found out a thousand times before by a thousand old women on buses?

While you're at it, avoid sets, too. When you only have ten sets in a decade, one for each year, it's tough for a set to get overlooked or bypassed. And anyway, sets are increasingly being viewed as a collection of stars plus a collection of everybody elses. The everybody elses don't do you any good unless you're a true collector and a real fan to boot. You're better off being mercenary and going for the collection of stars right off the bat.

The only possible exception to that advice is the 1960 Topps set. If you absolutely have to have a set out of the decade, this might be the one to have. At $4,000, it's no exceptional bargain, but it is less expensive than the sets on either side of it and it does have the rookie cards of Hall of Famers Willie McCovey and Carl Yastrzemski and the rookie card of possible Hall of Famer Jim Kaat (more on him later). There's nothing in this set that should make it $1,500 less than the 1961 set. Some of that gap is likely prejudice on the part of some people towards horizontal-format sets. Well, isn't that silly? I'd a hundred times rather have the horizontal '60s for all their grotesquely airbrushed caps and jerseys than the '59s, with their ping-pong-ball design. And the numbers bear me out: The '60 set has risen $600 in the last six months.

Single cards within the set you might want to check out in-

clude the second-year card of Bob Gibson (big drop down to $40),
cards of Hall of Fame managers Walt Alston ($6) and Al Lopez
($5), and the high-number all-star cards of Eddie Mathews ($30)
and Don Drysdale ($20). If you're a gambler and a believer that
anyone who wins 283 games and 16 Gold Gloves in a career that
spans four decades ought to be in the Hall of Fame, drop $30 on
the rookie card of Jim Kaat. But this is one of those rare instances
in the '60s where the set fares better than its individual cards.

No such luck in the 1961 set. Most of the key cards are in
place, and at about the same prices as in the 1960 set. This time
around the biggest cards are the rookies of Billy Williams ($125)
and Juan Marichal ($110)—not bad, either one of them. But the
kicker is a high-number set where even the most common cards
are $25 a throw. You're better off forsaking that set in favor of cards
like Stan Musial ($75) and Ernie Banks ($30). You might also want
to play gambler with the rookie card of Ron Santo ($35). He's
among the longest of long shots for Cooperstown, but his offensive
numbers are good enough to get him there.

There's also a 1961 Leaf set to consider. This black-and-white
set is a little short on big-name players but has some room to grow.
You could—and probably will—do worse on many of the Topps
set from the same time period.

The 1962 Topps set is blah-looking and high-priced. About
the only fun you can have with this set is by buying some of the
truly low-rent special cards like "Ford Tosses A Curve" ($6), "Kille-
brew Sends One Into Orbit" ($5), "Spahn Shows No-Hit Form"
($7), or "Musial Plays 21st Season" ($12). Remember, these aren't
true substitutes for star cards. But at these prices, they don't have
to be. Oh, and two more interesting cards: The Tony Oliva rookie
card, at $35, is a moderately priced first card of a borderline Vet-
erans Committee-type Hall of Famer; and the "Friendly Foes"
card, which shows Gil Hodges and Duke Snider, is really under-
priced at $6.50, especially when you consider what dealers are
getting for other cards of these two sentimental favorites.

The 1963 Fleer set is also interesting. It's a small set (66 cards)
and not really cheap ($1,000) and it came packaged with a cookie
(cookie crumbs, actually), but like all Fleer sets of the era it's really
tough to find in true Near Mint condition—clean, glossy and nicely

centered. Clean in particular. If you prefer to pass on the set, consider the single cards of Hall of Famers Brooks Robinson ($30), Bob Gibson ($30) and Roberto Clemente ($30). If nothing else, pick up the Jim Kaat card ($7) out of the set. When you figure out how much this set costs on a flat per-card rate and then figure out how much more expensive the star cards are in relation to the mean price of a card, the stars are real buys.

Topps convinced Fleer (with a pointed stick, ostensibly) as this set was being distributed that Fleer was better off sticking to Dubble Bubble and leaving the baseball cards to Topps, and so that was the end of Fleer sets for a while.

Lots of people like the 1964 Topps set, and it is cheap ($3,000). But that's its only real plus, outside of the relatively cheap high-numbered rookie card of Phil Niekro ($175), and, for the perversely speculative, the rookie card of Richie-Call-Me-Dick Allen, which is worth $10 alone on the notion that just like they will with Tony Oliva, someone at some time is going to recognize the most feared hitter in the National League through the '60s and early '70s and do something nice for him.

The '65 set is $500 more than the '64 set, but most of that is the Steve Carlton rookie card, which goes for $525 and is rising in anticipation of his Hall of Fame enshrinement. Funny thing, though: The same thing isn't happening to the Tony Perez card in the same set, which is about $375 cheaper and in a tough number series to boot. You're far better off with the Perez rookie instead of the Carlton rookie—or the whole set less the Carlton rookie, if you can get a dealer to sell it to you that way. True, if you buy the set you get Vic Roznovsky and Dick Wakefield, but you also get a manager card of Hall of Famer Billy Herman, the last cards of Warren Spahn and Casey Stengel, a Joe Morgan rookie and a Jim Hunter rookie. It's something to think about.

The 1966 Topps set is made interesting by a wicked high-number series that is full of short-prints (Choo Choo Coleman among them) and the cards of Hall of Famers Willie McCovey, Gaylord Perry and Billy Williams. The cards are definitely underpriced in relation to their scarcity, but they beg the question of whether anybody cares about their rarity relative to their scarcity. Is the average card investor type going to give two hoots that you have to search the world over for a good '66 McCovey or Williams? Probably not. It's their loss for their ignorance, but as long as it's their money driving the market, you're not going to benefit from their shortsightedness. Long-term may be a different story.

The '67 Topps set has another wicked high-number series full of Hall of Famers, including the Rod Carew and Tom Seaver rookies. Drat. Not that these cards would have been cheap under any circumstances, but their location takes them out of circulation for the average card buyer (though the Carew rookie at $475 isn't *that* far out of line) and forces him to look elsewhere in this set, where he finds. . .zilch. Okay, semi-zilch. Luis Aparicio for $5 and a slew of Hall of Famers clustered towards the end of the set, where the cards get less and less affordable. What's a mother to do?

Opt for the 1968 set, where the star cards that were in the high-number series come down the heights and actually feign affordability. And potential, even. Billy Williams for $7, Eddie Mathews for $10, Willie Stargell for $8, Don Drysdale for $8, Killebrew for $12, Wilhelm for $6, Carew for $150, Tom Seaver for $200. . .now think about those two cards for a moment. Back in the '67 set, Seaver goes for $1,200 and Carew for $475. Same number series. Same level of scarcity. But you come back down to the '68 set and the second-year Seaver is $200 while the second-year Carew is $150. Does this make sense? Of course not. But here's the $50 question: Is the Seaver rookie overvalued and the rest of the cards priced fairly, or is the Seaver second-year card undervalued? Or vice versa: Is the Carew rookie undervalued and the second-year card priced fairly, or is the second-year card overvalued? Hey, you can drive yourself batty trying to sort out this stuff. My guess is that the Seaver rookie's overvalued, but that wouldn't dissuade me in the least from going after that Carew rookie. There's some value there, too.

I think of the 1969 set—and the 1970 set, too—as a transitional set. These are the sets where you can finally ease up on the scrounging for mathematically undervalued Hall of Famer cards and start doing a little speculating on Hall of Famers to come. Not Reggie Jackson, of course; at $500, his rookie card's a little too dear, though you can't discount the possibility of its increasing 15 percent from there when he's elected into the Hall of Fame. But how about Craig Nettles in the 1969 set ($20)? He hit an awful lot of home runs, and though his batting average is nothing to write the folks about, he played great ball for some marquee teams, and has the reputation of being a big-play/big-game type of player. So you have to figure he has a shot, with the Veterans' Committee if nothing else. Bill Buckner, a heck of a hitter, has his rookie card in the 1970 set, and it's only $6. Is that worth a gamble—as much as Darrell Evans for $20 in the 1970 set? You'd think so.

Consider these cards while you're at it: The "Ted Shows How" card in the 1969 set, which features Senators manager Ted Williams and youngster Mike Epstein ($3.25); the Ted Williams card in that same set ($10, and a high number to boot); and the '69 "Giants Heroes" card, another high number that features Juan Marichal and Willie McCovey ($7). Collectors haven't caught on yet to any of these cards; as a result, they have headroom, and value.

The 1971 set has the potential to be one of the great sets of all time, sort of a modern-day 1952 Topps set. The reason? Its innovative use of action photos; its size (752 cards, the largest set to date); and its distinctive black borders, which make truly Near Mint cards very, very difficult to find.

While we have the opportunity, let's hit this grading thing hard. Especially with the '71s, but with all cards from this era, you really have to be demanding on grade. Make sure a card is nearly perfect before you pay a Near Mint price for it. If the gloss isn't there, if it's not perfectly centered—and centering is a big problem with cards from the '60s and '70s—if there are any sort of surface imperfections on it, or if it has gum or wax stains, don't pay the Near Mint price for it. Offer to buy it at an EX price—or less, depending on the degree of imperfection. You have to be demanding because the person you sell the card to, should you decide to sell, will be that demanding. This is no time to be a nice guy.

Insist on perfection with 1971 cards and you may have a bit of a search. But your diligence will be rewarded with cards that not only make the grade but also stand a far-better-than-average chance of increasing in value.

People have been focusing on the Bert Blyleven rookie card in the '71 set, but the card to really watch is the Ted Simmons rookie. Simba was a heck of a hitting catcher if much less than a heck of a fielding catcher, and if he does anything as general manager of the Pirates his Hall of Fame chances will be enhanced and his card, which is currently at $12 and holding, will really move.

I would seriously consider buying a truly Near Mint complete set at its $2,200 catalog value because of its toughness and the reputation it's beginning to develop among collectors. If you opt to go the single-card route with this set, consider the Dave Concepcion rookie at $10. Concepcion is a Veterans' Committee type who will get serious consideration for the Hall in another ten years. Also, the cheaper-than-cheap rookie cards of Bob Grich (a surprisingly good statistical second baseman, a winner, and a $2.25 rookie card); the Ted Williams manager card (a beautiful card, and only $5); and a tough high-number card of Roberto Clemente ($60, but you get what you pay for).

The '72 Topps set gets sort of weird designwise—the influence of Dr. Timothy Leary is found throughout—and has no great rookie cards outside of Carlton Fisk ($125), but has an in-action series that can make you think. Many of the best players of the day have regular cards and in-action cards side-by-side, with the in-action cards priced 50 percent to 60 percent less than the regular cards. This is not too far off from where they should be, but they're a good source of relatively inexpensive cards of Willie Mays ($10, versus $25 for his regular card), Harmon Killebrew ($2 versus $5), Johnny Bench ($15 versus $35), Reggie Jackson ($10 versus $35), Tom Seaver ($10 versus $25), Rod Carew ($40 versus $110), Pete Rose ($20 versus $40) and Roberto Clemente ($10 versus $25). Actually, both Clemente cards in this set are recommended. Clemente's regular '72 card is a beaut.

If the 1972 set is the card equivalent of "I Had Too Much to Dream Last Night," the 1973 set is the card equivalent of "Louie, Louie." Sort of grungy, sort of poorly played, not very musical at all. Topps' airbrushing was never worse and its stabs at action photos include a Joe Rudi card that shows everyone except Joe Rudi, a Luis Alvarado card that runs uphill, a Reggie Jackson card that was shot by Leroy Nieman with an Instamatic, a shot-to-the-groin Pat Corrales card and a Tommy Agee card that incorporates despicable airbrushing with a congregation of players, one of whom might be Tommy Agee. On the other hand, it does have the rookie cards of Rich Gossage ($12), Bob Boone ($35), Dwight Evans ($70) and Mike Schmidt ($450). Their chances for induction are directly proportional to the prices of their cards. Mike Schmidt is a lock, maybe unanimously so. Evans has the offensive and defensive credentials, and should make it in before Boone, who has longevity as his sole claim to fame. Gossage is the longest shot, but if Rollie Fingers can make it, so can Gossage—eventually. A lot depends on how the careers of Jeff Reardon, Lee Smith and Dennis Eckersley end up. The Hall of Fame, no matter what the year, will be loath to admit too many relievers.

Prices really drop off for sets starting with the 1973 set, and rightly so. They're dog sets. They're short on big-name rookie cards and they're practically interchangeable. But they are sets, and older sets, and tough to find in genuine Near Mint condition. For about $2,750 you can get a run of complete sets from 1974–79. That's the price of one card from the '50s; for that price, you get the rookie cards of Dave Winfield ('74 set; $80), Robin Yount ('75; $200), George Brett ('75; $200), Gary Carter ('75; $35), Dennis Eckersley ('76; $40), Andre Dawson ('77; $60), Dale Murphy ('77; $40), Eddie Murray ('78; $75), Paul Molitor and Alan Trammell ('78; $60), Jack Morris ('78; $10), Ozzie Smith ('79; $70), and Pedro Guerrero ('79; $10). You figure those thirteen cards will produce at least ten Hall of Famers; figure $100 for each of those cards—and that's conservative; look at what Yount and Brett rookies are selling for already—and that's $1,000. Figure $275 for each of those cards and you've made back your money on the sets, without factoring in another solitary card. There is money in these sets; take my word for it.

Before we dismiss these sets in a lump, a couple of notes. 1973 was the last year cards were issued in series; from 1974 on the concept of scarcity inside sets becomes moot. High numbers cease to exist in the manner they had before. Also, there's a miniversion of the 1975 set that was distributed almost solely in Michigan; it's $1,500, and undervalued right now. But while it's undervalued, it's an eccentric set. You have to ask yourself when you consider this set whether its most important physical feature, its small size, is so compelling that people will always want to pay significantly more for it.

BASKETBALL

Like the '50s, the '60s were not halcyon days for pro basketball or basketball cards. Not even close. The result is a limited number of sets—one, to be exact—with a big price tag and a tiny horizon. That's not to say the 1961–62 Fleer set is a dog. Far from it. When a set has the first cards of Oscar Robertson, Wilt Chamberlain, Elgin Baylor and Jerry West it doesn't go around sniffing tires. But outside of Len Wilkens at $35 there aren't any good buys in the set, the cards look like the faked-up black-and-white wirephotos that they are, and you can't even find clean, well-centered cards. It's not worth the trouble.

You're better off waiting for the '69–70 Topps set. Topps' return to basketball cards coincided with the arrival of Lew Alcindor, a/k/a Kareem Abdul-Jabbar, in the NBA. The cards are oversized but have never attracted the knock-down, drag-out adulation oversized football and hockey cards have received. The result? Outside of the can't-touch-these rookie cards of Alcindor ($850), John Havlicek ($125), and Senator Bill Bradley ($190), some genuine values. Try the Nate Thurmond rookie at $8.50. Thurmond was just elected to the Basketball Hall of Fame; his card's a real buy. Similarly are the first cards of Connie Hawkins ($10), Bill Cunningham ($25), Wes Unseld ($30), Willis Reed ($30), Don Nelson ($17.50) and Walt Frazier ($50).

The basketball-card market has made some tremendous strides pricewise in the last several years, but most of them have affected only the biggest names, like Jabbar, and Michael Jordan-era players. A Hall of Famer like Thurmond, or a legend like Hawkins, have been passed over in the shuffle. That shouldn't be seen as a permanent situation.

One of the biggest differences between basketball cards and baseball cards is the insignificance of Hall of Fame induction when it comes to a basketball player's card prices. The Basketball Hall of Fame covers college and professional ball; very often a so-so pro player, like Easy Ed McCauley, will be inducted into the Hall based on what he did cumulatively between college and the pros. And basketball-card buyers have never been keen on working a player's college background into the equation for valuing his pro card. So you can't use the Hall of Fame as a handy yardstick for measuring players. You have to rely on less tangible measures, like how a player is remembered across the country, to calculate how much a player's card ought to be worth. And if your calculations don't match everyone else's calculations, you're out of luck.

You still have to like the oversized '69-70 and '70-71 sets, though, as sets to invest in and sets to have. The '70-71 set in particular is worth every cent of its $1,200. There's even a scarce number set to deal with, not to mention the rookie cards of Pete Maravich ($150) and Pat Riley ($35).

The cards shrank in 1971-72, but while the cards shrank the set swelled, thanks to the addition of cards from the upstart rival league, the American Basketball Association. The ABA would never be treated with the equanimity accorded the American Football League, but the ABA received relatively separate-but-equal treatment from Topps. The red, white and blue ball and the afroed and love-beaded and mustachioed guys who shot it were a kick then and remain a source of enjoyment. Check out John Hester's necklace, George Peeples' hair or Wendell Ladner's mustache. Also check out the rookie cards of ABA greats Larry Brown ($7.50), Rick Barry ($75), Dan Issel ($17.50, and worth every penny), Roger Brown ($2), Mel Daniels ($2), and Doug Moe ($4). On the NBA side, the rookie card of workhorse center Bob Lanier ($17.50) is recommended over the cards of flashy Tiny Archibald ($19) and Dave Cowens ($30).

While Cowens' rookie doesn't get the nod, it does remind us of the cardinal rule of basketball cards, namely: Celtics sell. Knicks and Lakers do okay, especially on their respective coasts, but the Celtics are the Celtics and sell everywhere. Remember that; there'll be a test later.

The 1972-73 has lots of great second-year cards, an expensive rookie card in Julius Erving ($225, but who's to say it's overpriced, after what Erving meant to the pro game?), and a great rookie card in Artis Gilmore ($15). The shot-blocking center from

Jacksonville has never received his due, and wishing isn't going to make it so. A spectacular value nonetheless.

The '73-74 set has no big rookies (Bob McAdoo for $14?), but it does have some of the most gloriously low-rent photographs and design ever employed on cards. This is a card set where the overriding graphic element is the cement-block wall. That's where most of the players were posed, pretending to dribble a ball, faking a pass, or just standing there. It's a set you can buy for laughs and get your $260 worth.

In fact, you might as well buy all these '70s basketball sets. The game may not have been the NBA game of today, but the price is fantastic—between $75-$250 a set, and every set has Julius Erving and Kareem Abdul-Jabbar, plus the occasional rookie card of note (Bill Walton in the '74-75 set, $25; Moses Malone in the '75-76 set, $70; Adrian Dantley in the '77-78 set, $12; Robert Parish in the same set, $35; Alex English in the '78-80 set, $20). The fact that these players are either in the twilight of their careers or just retired makes this the time to buy these cards; they'll never be regarded in a less favorable light than they are now. From now on it's seashells and balloons and warm, fuzzy memories.

A set deserving special mention is the '76-77 set. It's not only oversized, it's supersized. The cards are about the same size as Topps' ill-fated Super baseball and football cards, only it's Topps' regular set for the year. Not surprisingly, it met the same fate as the Supers, but it's interesting to think that Topps thought so little of basketball cards that it gave gimmick-set treatment to the sport's only set. It was the sort of treatment that the NBA remembers every time basketball-license time comes around and Topps is at the door, hat in hand. Take a hike, kid.

FOOTBALL

Football cards are undoubtedly the most interesting sports cards of the '60s and '70s. There is more fun to be had with these cards, and more opportunities to have fun. There is also more money to be made buying up cards of good football players.

Football was the pre-eminent sport of the '60s and '70s. The names of its heroes trip off the tongue far more readily than the names of the era's top baseball players: Joe Namath, Johnny Unitas, Merlin Olsen, Roger Staubach, Terry Bradshaw, Franco Harris, Bob Griese, Paul Warfield, Larry Czonka, Jim Brown. The games and teams are likewise more memorable: the Ice Bowl, the Super Bowl, the Immaculate Reception, the Packers, the Steelers, and the Dolphins, the Cowboys. The Hall of Fame also means something in this sport; players' cards go up when they're enshrined, especially when the player being enshrined is a lineman or defensive back. These players can have common-priced cards before their enshrinement, and their cards can really shoot up once they're named to the Hall. Bob St. Clair is a perfect example. His cards were rattling around in the commons bins before he became a Hall of Famer; now his card's a $5 item. And that happens often enough that you ought to be expecting it and acting accordingly.

There were also more makers of football cards through this time, and more sets to be had. The result is a free-wheeling segment of the market where there are cards to buy for the ages and cards to speculate in whenever you have the urge.

It's ironic that the worst set of the era is the first. The 1960 Topps set has no rookie cards of note save for Forrest Gregg at $25, a handful of so-so second-year cards (Bobby Mitchell at $7.50, Sam Huff at $5) and a $650 price tag that's there for window dressing if nothing else. Better to go scrounging in the 1960 Fleer set, where a card of offensive whiz Sid Gillman is $10 but the first card of quarterback-turned-presidential-candidate-turned-cabinet-officer Jack Kemp is a hard-to-swallow $375. People are buying Kemp's card figuring he'll be elected president someday, but it doesn't look real promising for Jack. And what if he never gets there? Better off to bet on Hall of Fame induction than bet on the presidency.

In 1961 both Fleer and Topps made full NFL and AFL sets. The result is unprecedented choice, and scarce AFL series in both cases. The short-printed Fleer AFL cards are almost twice as scarce as the Topps AFL cards, and the Fleer set is a condition rarity to boot. If you can find a clean, well-centered, slightly glossy set of these cards at anywhere near their $1,300 price tag, snap them up. If you knew the cards you'd know how hard they are to find in top grade. Especially recommended are the Fleer rookie cards of Don Maynard ($65), ironman center Jim Otto ($40) and the first card of Hall of Fame possible Johnny Robinson ($7.50).

In 1962 Topps took the NFL and Fleer the AFL, and the result was two outstanding sets. The Fleer set is actually under-priced at $550, even with no key rookies, given how hard it is to find clean Fleer cards. The '62 Topps set has hellacious black borders, the rookie cards of Fran Tarkenton ($450) and Mike Ditka ($100), some nasty shortprints and a killer reputation among collectors. As a value judgment, the set probably isn't worth its $1,700 price tag; on the other hand, if you find a set with absolutely pristine black borders, you probably ought to snap it up in an instant. True Near Mint examples of this set are almost impossible to find.

The '63 Fleer set suffers from the same problems all Fleer sets do: Bad printing and scarcity. Extra scarcity, in this case: Fleer stuck cards of two players, Charlie "Choo Choo" Long and Bob Dougherty, at the absolute end of the press run. Their cards are not found on every sheet; as a result, they're ultra-scarce. One big-name dealer whom I won't name because he probably wouldn't like it known that he dabbles in football cards says the Dougherty and Long cards are the toughest he's ever had to track down in all his years of collecting and dealing. The other cards in the set aren't exactly common as chuckholes, either, and there are some significant ones, like the rookie cards of Lance Alworth ($150) and Len Dawson ($165). The '63 Topps set comes off bland by comparison. Though it features the first cards of Hall of Famers Willie Wood ($30), Ray Nitschke ($54), Bob Lilly ($85), Larry Wilson (recommended at $25), and Deacon Jones ($50), and affordable cards of Hall of Famers Ray Berry ($5.35), Jim Parker ($4.75), Gino Marchetti ($5), Jim Ringo ($4.75) and Bob St. Clair ($5).

Starting in 1964, Topps revised its AFL/NFL split, taking the AFL and leaving the NFL to a newcomer: Philadelphia Gum, which had never done a set before and would never do any other major sets outside of the four football sets it issued from 1964 to 1967. The Philly sets share clean lines and classic styling; they're also extremely affordable. Since these sets were issued about the time the AFL began stealing some serious thunder from the NFL—not to mention some serious players—these sets aren't exactly dripping with rookies. But the three or four each set provides are big names, and the great players scattered throughout are still great players.

For instance, the '64 Philly set has the first football cards of Hall of Famer John Mackey ($10), Don Sula ($15), Willie Davis ($35), Herb Adderley ($35), Vince Lombardi (a more-than-affordable $30, even if it's only a cameo on one of Philly's hokey play-of-the-year cards), Merlin Olsen ($75), and all-time-great Viking center Mick Tinglehoff ($3.50, and it ought to be a lot more). Now, that's not Joe Namath or anything, but it's a nice array of rookie cards to go along with the Starrs and Unitases and Jimmy Browns. The next year's Philly set has the first cards of Paul Warfield ($50), Carl Eller ($8.50, ugly, but underpriced), Charley Taylor ($40) and Paul Krause (bargain at $3). Again, a nice selection, but nothing real revolutionary. Same with Dick Butkus ($150), Gale Sayers ($250) and Bob Hayes ($3—what a value!) the next year. Good cards, reasonably priced sets, bargains among the singles: These are the sorts of sets you like to see, both as a collector and a card buyer. They make collecting older cards fun.

The Topps sets from the same era, unfortunately, pose a few more obstacles to the collector. The '64 and '65 sets are full of short prints, which make completing a set difficult. Who completes sets anymore, though? And since the short-prints are hardly ever stars, prices for the cards you're likely to want aren't going to be affected.

The '64 set doesn't have any big-name rookies, but it's a nice set that collectors want, and worth its $1,650 price tag. The '65 set is probably the most famous and sought-after set of football cards this side of the '53 Bowman large cards. The oversized, colorful cards represent the apex of football-card design, which may not say much about football-card design but proves that you don't have to be fancy to make great football cards. The set is aided immeasurably by the presence of the Joe Namath rookie, as otherworldly a football card as you're likely to find, though the set also contains rookie cards of Ben Davidson ($22.50, sans mustache) and Fred Biletnikoff ($150, sans long stringy hair). The '66 Topps set's scarcest card is—no kidding—a funny-ring checklist. (The rings were bonus items in packs.) Outside of resurrecting the '55 Bowman baseball TV borders, the '66 Topps set is remarkable for the rookie card of Otis Taylor ($10), a sure-to-be Hall of Famer and about as safe a bet along those lines as you're likely to find. The '67 set has zilch for rookie cards, but it's affordable ($475) almost to the point of being underpriced. The cards also have plugs for AFL football on NBC on their backs, the first time football cards were used as an advertising vehicle for something more than the company's candy—but not the last time.

When the rival leagues joined forces so did their football cards. Philadelphia Gum simply stopped making cards and Topps was left with a monopoly again, and if things got less interesting from that point on, well, that's just the nature of a monopoly. It's to Topps' credit that football cards stayed interesting through the '60s and well into the '70s. Only in the late '70s did things begin to deteriorate and sets start to get boring.

Nothing boring about the '68 Topps set. In addition to the rookie cards of borderline Hall of Famers Jim Hart ($5) and Floyd Little ($5), the set has the first NFL card of Canadian Football League Hall of Famer Joe Kapp ($2.50) and the ever-so-slightly overpriced rookie card of Bob Griese ($85). In addition, Packer and Raider cards share a unique horizontal design in an unheralded tribute to the teams of Super Bowl I, and all Hall of Famers save for the biggest names can be had for $6.50 or less.

You can apply a little of the how-come philosophy we applied to baseball sets to the 1969 and '70 Topps football sets. The 1969 set has one big rookie—Larry Csonka ($65)—and sells for $525, while the 1970 set has at least ten big-name rookies, some Hall of Famers, some borderline guys and some interesting cases, yet it sells for $450. Do you smell a bargain here? Actually, you do. That $450 gets you the rookie cards of O.J. Simpson ($175), Jan Stenerud ($7.50), Bubba Smith ($15), Tom Mack ($4), Alan Page ($20), Harold Jackson ($4.50), Lem Barney ($9), Bill Bergey ($4), Fred Dryer ($12.50), and Calvin Hill ($3.50). This is a set with loads of potential, and a set to buy if you're shopping. If you can't afford the entire set, go for the rookie cards—all of them, even Simpson. They have room to grow.

When you get to the '71 set, the bigger name rookies—Terry Bradshaw ($150), Ken Houton ($15) and Willie Lanier ($15)—

have big-name price tags, but some good guys with Hall of Fame-type numbers, like Roger Wehrli ($1.50), Charle Sanders ($2.50) and Jake Scott ($1.50), are cheap. It's an overpriced set compared to the '70 set, but it's attractive and interesting—qualities that grow increasingly scarce as you move through the decade.

But not to worry about the 1972 Topps set. It's the most interesting American set of the decade, and on pure strangeness, maybe the most interesting American set ever made. The design is nothing special, neat and clean, and the rookie cards are ample, solid and straightforward (John Riggins, $20; Archie Manning, $10; Jim Plunkett, $15; Ted Hendricks, $15; L.C. Greenwood, $10; Lyle Alzado, $15; Roger Staubach, $125; Charlie Joiner, $17.50). There's a truly horrid in-action series that gives us the first glimpse of what would become Topps' trademark through the decade: airbrushed helmets that make players look like they were wearing golf balls, yo-yos or mushrooms on their heads, and painted-over jerseys that look like they could have been done with fingerpaints. And hair. Lots of long hair. The NFL discovered hair starting with the 1972 set.

All that's well and good and fairly interesting, but what's *really* interesting are the packs and series. Topps used seven or eight different colored packs for the year and issued its cards in three series. Most of the country only saw two of the series, though. Almost the entire third series was bought up by Larry Fritsch, a major card dealer, and only a limited amount of cards were distributed to stores—almost all of them in central Wisconsin. As a result, if you didn't buy the third series from Larry Fritsch you weren't likely to get it. The result has been outlandish prices—$7.50 per card and up—for third-series cards. The ultra-expensive has driven the price for the entire set up to $1,900—an incredible sum, given that the sets on either side of it are $550 and $450, respectively. You don't buy this set; you regard it, from a distance.

Once you get past the 1973 set things descend into boredom quickly. The '73 set is a bargain because of its proximity to the way-too-interesting '72 set and because of its plethora of good rookies. The '73 set has Hall of Famers, soon-to-be Hall of Famers, and wanna-bes Ken Anderson ($20), Art Shell ($25), Franco Harris ($55, in a godawful hat), Jack Ham ($17.50), Dan Dierdorf

($12.50, and a legitimate Hall of Famer), Jim Langer ($12.50), Jack Youngblood ($10), and Ken Stabler ($20). The '73 rookie class is easily the best class of the rest of the '70s, and the set prices show it. They roll off rapidly once you get past this set, with a blip for the 1976 set and its rookie card of Walter Payton ($175).

You can buy the whole bloody lot of football sets from 1974–79 if you want for one low price, but you're better off doing a little romping and rolling and cherry-picking. First and foremost, hey, we know how great Walter Payton and Steve Largent were, and so if you want their rookie cards based on greatness alone, fine. Go ahead and spend the money for the Payton and the Largent ($85). The Payton in particular might actually be worth some of that money. But consider also the second-year Payton or the rookie card of certain HOFer Mike Webster ($5). Granted, Mike Webster is hardly the marquee name Steve Largent has been, but time is going to dim that marquee somewhat. In fifteen years what people are going to know of Largent and Webster is that they're both Hall of Famers. So spend $15 for Mel Blount or $15 for Joe Theismann or $4.50 for Cliff Branch. Spend a whopping 75 cents each for Harvey Martin rookies. Ten dollars for a Too Tall Jones rookie and only 75 cents for Harvey Martin? It doesn't seem quite right. Spend $4 a shot for Ray Guy rookies. When he becomes the first pure punter inducted into the Hall of Fame you'll thank me. Buy some later cards of great players. The last Unitas card is $12.50 in the '74 set. Charley Taylor is $1.50 in the same set. Ted Hendricks is $2.50 and Jim Otto $2. In the 1976 set Joe Greene is $2.50 and Len Dawson $2.50. George Blanda is $4.50. John Hannah is $1. Buy these cards. They're great cards for the years ahead, believe me.

Let us not leave the decade without mentioning the 1979 Earl Campbell card. Hall of Famer Campbell didn't appear on many cards, and this one is his very first. It's $27, but it's like buying a Stan Musial card: Everybody wants one, no one can understand why there aren't more, and the price goes up as a result. Also, very quickly: The John Stallworth rookie for $10 in the '78 set. The James Lofton rookie for $30 in the '79 set. The entire '79 set for $125. Buy it and don't quit. It ends the decade on a very positive note.

HOCKEY

If you're looking to buy a hockey set from the '60s, two words of advice: Forget it. Hockey sets from the 1960s are among the most tightly priced cards of all. Like hockey cards of the '50s, '60s hockey cards are intensely collected. Supplies are not adequate to meet demand. The few sets that show up on the market sell quickly, and for straight book prices. This is great news if you have sets to sell. If you're looking to buy sets, however, this combination makes for tough buying. You have to spend so much to get a set that you might as well buy an annuity, for all the explosive growth it'll get you. So don't buy hockey sets from the '60s. Fortunately, some of the values within sets loosen up enough that you can actually make a few buys that might net you a little change while providing you with cards of good players. Be prepared to spend $25 and up for these prizes, though.

A couple of notes on the hockey sets of the '60s, because they can get confusing. Topps and Parkhurst continued their Boston-New York-Chicago/Montreal-Toronto-Detroit tradeoff until Parkhurst got fed up with the card business (no kidding!) and suspended its card operations after the 1963–64 season. Its last set is a beauty; it's priced like one ($2,400), but you can afford a couple of cards out of the set: Red Kelly ($40), Toe Blake ($40) and Dave Keon ($35). Keon, along with Norm Ullman, are two of the great hockey players of the era whose cards approach affordability. Over the Topps side, players like Jean Ratelle ($40), Rod Gilbert ($40), Jacques Plante ($50), Glenn Hall ($40), Doug Harvey ($35) and Andy Bathgate ($25) at least show some pretend affordability. It's cards of excellent players such as these where the value, such as it is, lies with the '63–'64 sets.

In 1966–67 Topps began targeting sets to the U.S. market. Its first U.S. set was a test issue, and the Bobby Orr rookie out of that set is the most valuable hockey card of the era, and perhaps the most valuable hockey card of all. For the 1968–69 season Topps turned its Canadian hockey operation over to its licensee, O-Pee-Chee, and focused its attention on the American hockey-card market. The O-Pee-Chee sets throughout the remainder of the decade and on into the '70s are larger than the American Topps sets, contain more key rookies and are more sought after by collectors. They're also more expensive, more aggressively collected and harder to find.

As mentioned in passing a couple of paragraphs ago, your strategy with 1960s hockey sets should be to buy the cards of key players with at least some name recognition. Unlike football and baseball, where Hall of Fame enshrinement provides the necessary name recognition for players who excelled in the shadows, hockey has a Hall of Fame that's as low-profile as the sport. As a result, if the player doesn't have a recognizable name to a hockey fan, you might as well forget his cards. They're not going anywhere. You can also see why it pays to be a hockey fan if you want to buy hockey cards.

Players that fit the bill from the '60s sets include Johny Bucyk, whose cards normally sell in the $25 range; Gump Worsley, the cult-favorite goalie, whose cards start at about $40; Rod Gilbert, Vic Hadfield and Jean Ratelle, the Rangers' top line of the late '60s and early '70s; Dave Keon and Norm Ullman; Andy Bathgate; Henri "The Pocket Rocket" Richard, the Montreal forward whose cards can be found for around $35 each; Stan Mikita, who has a few cards that descend from the stratosphere into the $50 to $75 range; and Frank Mahovlich, the prolific scorer whose cards start at about $50. These players' cards can also be tracked well into the '70s, if you want.

Actually, by the time you get to the 1968-69 Topps hockey set you can see a few changes. The set is down to $600, and though that $600 gets you no one, it's a set of hockey cards from the '60s and includes some affordable cards of Terry Sawchuk ($15) and Jean Beliveau ($10). The same thing holds in the '69-70 set, where a Gordie Howe card is $75 and the rookie card of Serge Savard is an affordable $30.

You can even start speculating—gasp!—on a few players in the '70s sets. The sets are more affordable—less than $1,000 each across the board—and more available. But given the prevailing collect-at-all-costs philosophy of many hockey-card collectors, it might not be a bad idea to stock up on as many of these sets—the O-Pee-Chee versions, if you can find them—as you can track down.

The last cards of the '60s gently address the NHL's changed

face. Expansion had come to the NHL, and with it, more hockey towns and more cities where hockey cards could be sold. Topps upped its press run beginning in 1968, and the result was more hockey cards. Maybe too many hockey cards, in retrospect. Topps found out what the NHL found out: Many Americans were just not yet ready to become hockey fans and hockey-card collectors, and hockey was not quite ready to become a sport as big as football or basketball. But hockey was fundamentally changed by the expansion of the late '60s, and that became most apparent in the hockey cards of the early '70s.

As the game opened up to expansion, players who might not have gotten a break in the six-team tightness of the '60s found stardom: Gilbert Perreault ($50 in the '70-71 OPC set), Bobby Clarke ($110 in the '70-71 OPC set), Bill Smith ($45 in the '73-74 set) and Dennis Potvin ($60 in the 1974-75 set) all got their breaks on expansion teams, and the diluted talent pool made it possible for players like Marcel Dionne ($125 in the 1971-72 set) and Darryl Sittler ($40 in the '70-71 set), and international stars like Borje Salming ($20 in the 1974-75 OPC set) to get their breaks. All these cards, even Dionne, are good buys. They represent the rookie cards of the changing of hockey's guard, and that makes them exceptional buys. Also recommended out of these sets: the Larry Robinson rookie in the 1973-74 OPC set ($40), the Lanny McDonald rookie (1974-75 OPC; $40), the first card of coach and analyst Don Cherry (1974-75 OPC; $5), and the rookie card of Bruins favorite Terry O'Reilly ('73-74 OPC; $6). The '73-74 ($400) and '74-75 OPC ($300) sets are also recommended.

OPC went overboard from 1974-78 printing sets for the fledgling World Hockey Association. As a result, the sets, except for the '75-76 set (recommended at $300) are easy to find and cheap. They're also notable for their inexpensive cards of Jacques Plante ($7.50), Gordie Howe ($25-$35) and Bobby Hull ($25), and the rookie cards of players like Ulf Nilsson ($2) and Anders Hedberg ($2).

Looking for a good buy out of this mess? The 1978-79 OPC set has the rookie cards of Mike Bossy ($50), Bernie Federko ($7.50, and recommended), Doug Wilson ($10), Brian Sutter ($3.50) and Dave Taylor ($20), and it's only $175. Much better that than the 1979-80 OPC set, which goes for $900 on the strength of one card—the Wayne Gretzky rookie.

A friend of mine called me several months ago from Minneapolis, where he lives. He said he had a chance to buy a Wayne Gretzky rookie for around $550 and wanted to know whether I thought it was a good idea. I said no. It's not that I don't like Gretzky or the Gretzky rookie, or hockey cards in particular. I do. But my friend was thinking of buying the card strictly as a long-term investment—put the kids through college—and I don't like the card as a long-term investment. Sure, Gretzky is the greatest hockey player ever, but that's not like being the greatest football player or baseball player ever. The appeal of Gordie Howe, the previous greatest player ever, ain't what it used to be, and there's no reason to believe anything different for Gretzky, charismatic as he is. And for that card to go up the 10 percent to 15 percent a year that he expects, the card would have to be worth somewhere around $2,000 by the time he cashes it in. And sorry, but I don't think it's going to happen. And the card's been counterfeited too well and too many times for my tastes, too.

What did I recommend to my friend? Joe DiMaggio-signed baseballs. And he couldn't be happier.

The Sport Card Explosion—1980s

The eighties brought to the card hobby something never seen to an extreme like this before—an extended period of explosive growth. Sure, all collectibles cycle through periods of expansion and contraction, but in a few short years the card collecting hobby broke through the top of the curve. What was once a relatively minor hobby became a goldmine for some and a passion for many more, and as card companies burst onto the scene it seemed that every corner held a ma-and-pa-sized card shop to handle their wares.

Expansion? No, explosion was the better term. But the explosion came about only after competition breached the card market at the start of the decade. Ever since the demise of Bowman back in 1955, sports cards had been issued by Topps, and virtually only by Topps. The contracts Topps negotiated with the players shown on its cards were, in practice, exclusive contracts; by appearing on Topps cards, the players gave up their rights to appear on another company's cards. What it meant, of course, is that there were, virtually, no other company's cards, as the monopoly-in-practice that Topps maintained kept the market free from major competition for a full quarter decade.

Still, other companies eyed this market, most notably the Fleer Corp., a candy maker with some earlier card experience, and in a series of anti-trust court battles ending in 1980 Fleer finally succeeded in breaking Topps's monopolistic hold.

The spring of 1981 brought some anticipation to card collectors. Topps cards would be there; heck, Topps cards were always there. But what would the new Fleer cards be like? Would stores stock them? Would anyone want to collect them?

We waited . . . or at least a few of us did. But when the first non-Topps cards arrived: they weren't Fleer cards at all, but something called Donruss, an unknown brand made by Leaf, Inc. These Donruss cards were, in fact, the first competitor's cards to reach the shelves. I found Fleer cards only a few days later and bought a few packs of each.

They were baseball cards, alright, but they weren't good cards, in a quality sense. While the Topps monopoly was no more, these new producers soon learned that to make more than a temporary dent in the marketplace, they'd have to produce a better product. The earliest Fleer and Donruss products were truly dreadful—error-laden monstrosities with fuzzy, off-center photographs that were good for more laughs than anything we'd seen in years, even including some of the hilarious Topps airbrushed caps we knew each set would bring. Fleer's Kurt Bevacqua card has an error so obvious I couldn't stop staring at it when I pulled it from the pack—the reversed-negative photo showed the strangest Pirates hat I'd ever seen, a backwards "P" in bright gold on the normal black background.

It was the neatest wrong baseball card since the Topps "Washington Nat'ls" cards back in 1974. All told, the errors in these new sets numbered in the dozens, and many variations exist in these early Fleer and Donruss sets, including cards of what were then some of the game's biggest stars: Steve Carlton, Tom Seaver, George Foster, Steve Garvey and Pete Rose, among many.

But a handful of minor errors wasn't what the card explosion was about. Competition was the first key ingredient to the mix, since cardmakers now had a reason to go out and promote their products, to try to pull new buyers into the fold. Topps was still the biggie, and

Fleer and Donruss held onto relatively minor market shares. Yet the hobby needed more than just competition to explode. It needed exposure, and it needed a catalyst. And as the eighties matured, those factors joined the fun.

The exposure the card hobby needed really matched the increased exposure of national sports. If you were a baseball fan in the seventies, your only chance to watch a game on TV was Saturday afternoon, usually a network game featuring the Reds, Mets or Dodgers. But with the advent of the electronics age—meaning three color TVs and a cable connection or a satellite dish in every home—baseball and the other sports were available on a daily basis. Radio was fine for many, and to this day many still listen to more ballgames than they watch, but TV reached another audience. Cable brought Harry Caray's gravelly descriptions of the lovable but pathetic Cubbies to much of the nation, and down Atlanta way Ted Turner's new "Superstation," WTBS, was promoting the Braves as "America's Team." This meant that some soon hated the Braves as much as they hated the Cowboys, which was unfair to the Braves because they really weren't that good anyway, just sort of stumbling their way into a pennant the one year.

ESPN joined the fun, and soon negotiated rights to televise major league games. Many teams established or expanded already-existing regional networks as well, and you know what? Ballgames were everywhere. Ingredient two was well stirred.

The third ingredient was the catalyst, and his name was Donald Arthur Mattingly, the young, sweet-swinging first baseman for the Yankees. To say that the card hobby went from nowhere to the top of the heap in a few short years is not quite true; there have always been collectors of cards, and there have always been regions where card collecting was more popular. The Northeast was one of those areas (New York and Boston, mainly), and with the arrival of Mattingly and the sudden appearance of so many sports collectibles, the hobby got the boost it needed. Sometimes, when a process is started it picks up steam on its own. Cards did that. Mattingly was a made-to-order hero who fit well with the Yanks, both in the harsh atmosphere of the New York glare and as a part of that proud Yankee tradition—Ruth, Gehrig, Mantle, DiMaggio . . . all of them. You know the names. Mattingly put up the marquee stats. He hit .320 all the time, .352 in

1986. He'd hit 30 homers most years and drive in 110, although in 1985 he went nuts and knocked in 141. He led the league in doubles three straight years, with a high of 53. Great ballplayer, indeed. And two other things besides—he was handsome (or at least photogenic) . . . and he was white.

Said plainly enough? It wasn't the little black kids in Bedford-Stuyvesant who were snapping up the suddenly-popular Mattingly cards, and while cultural blinders might be appropriate for something as mild as a baseball card, the truth is that without Mattingly's skin color being what it was, the card explosion might not have happened as it did. Mattingly wasn't the only great Yankee player of the time. Those mid-'80s Bombers also had Rickey Henderson, only recently getting his due as the best leadoff hitter of the modern age, and Dave Winfield, a truly great ballplayer in his own right who could never rid himself of the stigma of his combative relationship with Yankee owner George Steinbrenner. The Steinbrenner/Winfield feud at times rivaled the Steinbrenner/Billy Martin one, which while normal doings for the Bronx Zoo meant that Winfield never had the chance to reach the "hero" status that Mattingly soon attained.

Why not Winfield? No particular reason stands clear. He was every bit the ballplayer Mattingly was, even if his "marquee stats" had a slightly different shape. The two of them waged a tremendous battle for the '84 AL batting title that Mattingly pulled out on the season's final day—and their were some racial overtones even in that, and in terms of overall skill, they matched up well. Henderson? He was easy enough to dismiss. Rickey's been a hero to damn few people besides Rickey's mom and Rickey himself, and his me-first attitudes have always clashed with the team concept cherished by fans and baseball people alike. Mattingly, though, was the Steve Garvey of the '80s, even if an excellent ballplayer instead of just an overrated good one. Mattingly it was: the catalyst the hobby needed.

But not even black vs. white is black-and-white, and while Mattingly was the biggest, there were other new and collectible names as well. Secondary boosts came from a number of stars making bold, splashy appearances about this time. So often the game of baseball produces waves of certain ballplaying types, and in the early and mid-'80s the stars' names were changing. Gone were the Roses and Garveys and Jacksons and Yaztrzemskis, and in their place came new players, often with new combinations of skills. Wade Boggs burst onto the Boston scene with feet of clay and hands of stone (he still can't run, but the defense has improved), with a swing that sent singles to all fields and a large number of opposite-field doubles off the easily-reached Green Monster. Henderson's stolen base and power exploits caught the eyes of many, and players like Vince Coleman followed in the media glare, though Coleman soon proved that stealing bases is a great talent, but only if you can get to first to begin with. Darryl Strawberry arrived at Shea Stadium with talent exceeded only by the expectations placed upon him. He was supposed to be Ty Cobb, the Babe, and Jesus all rolled into one, but by the longest of long shots he only turned out to be a great ballplayer instead. And Kirby Puckett and Jose Canseco and Will Clark and Tony Gwynn, and every team suddenly had new stars.

The game changed. . .subtly, but it changed. A huge wave of 40-something pitchers with 20-something big-league seasons and 300-something wins under their belts worked their way out of the bigs. Relief pitching and the art of saving games took on new importance. And about new, young starters? By some strange coincidence the two biggest pitching stars to arrive were in the two biggest card markets, New York and Boston. They weren't just the biggest names; they were the two best young pitchers on the scene. Rocket Roger Clemens arrived in Boston fresh from the University of Texas and immediately overpowered the AL, and back at Shea Stadium a 19-year-old rookie named Dwight "Doctor K" Gooden struck out batter after batter and went 41-13 his first two years. Arm and personal woes eventually shortened "Doctor K" to plain old "Doc," but to this day he remains a gutsy pitcher who knows how to win.

The game changed, as did the players, and the card hobby rode along. Always back to the cards. What are cards, anyway? Pieces of inked cardboard? Memories of a sunny Sunday afternoon? Tangible but difficult-to-liquidate investments on which we should all bet the ranch? They're a bit of all that, but really, they're plain old fun before anything else. Each collector, though, has his own reason for owning cards. There was the increased exposure of the game, there were new stars to cherish, and there were dollars—many, many dollars— to be made. The card collecting hobby exploded—in all sports, eventually, though baseball was first and remains the biggest.

There were those three companies making cards, Topps, Fleer, and Donruss. After those early disasters both Fleer and Donruss improved their cards' quality and became stable players, if still minor compared to Topps. Topps made many secondary sets, Fleer and Donruss just a few. In other sports, Topps made football cards, and while the NFL was always there the USFL came and went, leaving two then-worthless sets in its wake. NFL cards weren't much better, but Topps put them out every year. Nobody even made basketball cards after 1981, when Topps gave up on it, until Fleer took a chance on the expanding hobby with an issue for the '86–87 season. Hockey collectors had only Topps or O-Pee-Chee cards, which was never easy to obtain. Fortunately, not many collectors were trying to obtain them, or the roads to Sasketchewan would have been littered with the rusting carcasses of dead-on-the-pilgrimage Ford LTD station wagons. Or maybe old VW beetles, since parts for those were getting hard to find.

When did the hobby first expand? 1986? A good guess, but the signs must have been there in '85 because Topps made many more of its '86 cards than in previous years. By '87 the other companies had followed suit, and by the following season the suddenly wide-open hobby virtually extended a "WELCOME" mat to other companies waiting to enter. In '88 the next new brand appeared, a set of 660 "Score" cards from a company named Major League Marketing, Inc. Something new—a company in business to make cards, rather than a company in business, as with Topps, Fleer, and Leaf (Donruss), to make products for kids. This was a subtle but important difference. But like most new issues, the first Score cards weren't much good either.

Oh, and the rookie craze, and the error craze, and the diversity of the market into regular- and premium-grade collectibles. . .why, 1988 and 1989 seemed to produce a craze of the month, every month without question. The evaluation of rookie cards to investment-level status is a recent phenomenon. Why a George Brett card from 1975 should be worth eight or ten times as much as a George Brett card from 1977, when both exist in roughly equal quantities and conditions, is, when you look at it closely, a real, real, real good question. The climb of rookie card prices seems to have developed as a way of "grandfathering" baseball and baseball-card knowledge to "wise" investors: if you could see that Billy Suchand-such would be a great ballplayer a year before anyone else, than you should be rewarded for your incredible wisdom and foresight and your willingness to tuck the kids' college fund into Billy Suchandsuch futures. Like all collectibles, cards have precious little intrinsic value. Even that '52 Topps Mantle with the ninety-kajillion dollar price tag: what it is, really, is a chunk of cardboard—not even good cardboard, mind you—with a colored drawing of a ballplayer printed on it. It is worth exactly what someone else would pay you for it, no more and no less. Owning the card might be a great memory, and it's sure something that a lot of people want, or else the price wouldn't be so high. But buying that card because you like Mantle? You could proba-bly meet Mantle a whole lot cheaper. And because you bought his card Mickey's still not likely to drop by your place for a nice reminis-cence over tea and crumpets. If it's a memory it's a damned expensive one.

But don't think that cards are therefore worthless—they're ex-actly as valuable as many other things around us and sometimes more volatile.

Error cards are among the most volatile. Error cards went through a craze, spearheaded by the appearance in '89 of a Fleer Billy Ripken card with a nasty word in plain view. The card went from worthless to $100 in about two weeks, then went through a reality-adjustment phase and has been sliding back ever since. Today it's maybe a $5-10 card. Other error cards ignited similar runs, but a funny thing happened on the way to the gas mart: every set seemed to have a few errors that needed correcting, thereby creating "scarce" (and therefore "valuable") variations. This in turn meant that the boxes and packs holding these variations should just leap off the shelves and into the buyer's hands. Gee, seems like the people who stood to make the most from this are the people who made the cards in the first place. I'm a trusting soul (no, really I am!), but in this case it's plain to see that at least the **motive** for "accidentally" making an error did exist. Did it happen? None can say, or point to specifics. But the sudden onslaught of errors in the late '80s (and early '90s) and the cardmakers' sudden willingness to correct them makes one wonder . . .

Which brings us to market diversity, the last big development of the '80s. With expansion of the market came diversity, and the products available seemingly overnight meant a set of cards for almost everyone's taste. First up was the expansion or return to the other major sports—football first, than basketball and hockey—and then came diversification among the card types themselves. Where once baseball cards were just that—plain ol' cards—1989 brought the arrival of the first "premium-grade" brand, Upper Deck.

Upper Deck cards cost twice as much as their competitors, and in return offered a higher quality card. While cards for the high-end collector had existed for several years (Topps was foremost in this area, issuing what became known as their "Tiffany" sets, a limited-printing, special-production set), Upper Deck was the first to wed the higher-grade card to the mass-marketing approach. It was the best card available, and it was there for anyone to buy. Upper Deck was so successful that today every cardmaker issues at least one premium-grade brand, and several companies have abandoned the cheaper types altogether. It may or may not be what collectors needed, but it was most certainly what they wanted.

It was a wild decade. Ten years full of crazy developments and new sets by the hundreds. There are sets and cards already so expensive that only the wealthiest collectors can afford them, and there are cards so cheap and common that no one wants them. Both good buys and bad buys abound. Each of the four major sports has plenty to offer in the way of cards, and sport by sport, there's plenty of items that the "wise" collector can consider.

BASEBALL

Topps

Topps baseball sets during the decade range from the pre-competition 1980 set (a $275 buy) to the all but valueless '88 and '89 issues ($15 each). The '80 set climbs and falls with the fortunes of its single big rookie card, that of Rickey Henderson (#482). Though pricey at $125, the card may still have room to climb, given Rickey's overall abilities and the chance that his career stolen base total should pass 1,300 before he's through. The only other rookie card in the set worth consideration is that of Dan Quisenberry, the fine Royals reliever, whose card can be had for $1.75. Quisenberry is a long, long shot to make the Hall, but he was clearly the best reliever in baseball for several years and might sneak in through the memories of the Veterans Committee.

The '81 Topps set features no rookies of Henderson's stature, but the best rookie card it does hold—Tim Raines, #479—is a far better buy. This card is a steal at $8 and accurately reflects the degree to which Raines has been underrated throughout his career. Raines has played in Rickey's shadow throughout his career and it continues here: the Raines card is only second priciest in the set, trailing Henderson's **second**-year card. Jeff Reardon's rookie card is another on the list of best buys (#456, $7), as he passed Rollie Finger's career saves mark. Reardon is probably Hall-ward bound, but if you must bet the ranch there's an even better bet in the next Topps set, the '82s.

That card is the Lee Smith rookie, perhaps the best buy today of all early-'80s cards. The Topps version costs about $5, up from only $1 two short seasons ago, and it's a card destined to go much higher. Smith lags slightly behind Reardon in career saves but will someday pass him. He's two years younger, has only a few less saves, has posted lower ERAs and better strikeout/walk totals (while pitching in arguably worse parks for most of his career), and will be pitching after Reardon is gone from the game. Compare Smith's card and Cooperstown chances against those of George Bell (#254, $10); Bell no longer has a legitimate chance of compiling slugger's HOF-type totals. Don Baylor is the best level Bell can reach. Almost forgotten is the **other** rookie card here, that of Cal Ripken, Jr., whose card (#21) is a steady climber at $70. Another fine card, and overall, at $140, this '82 set is a tough value to beat.

The 1982 season also marked the first appearance of Topps's "Traded" sets, those 132-card year-end summaries of traded and rookie ballplayers. This '82 set is $200 or more, and while it has a very rare Ripken card within it, it goes less recommended here.

The star rookie card of 1983 is certainly Ryne Sandberg, who, like Ripken, could quit playing today and waltz into Cooperstown on the basis of what he's already done. Both will turn out to be ridiculously overqualified for enshrinement, but the Sandberg card—#83, $50 today—might turn out to be a better buy. Ripken's the slightly more potent offensive player and has his consecutive-games-played streak, while Sandberg added great speed to the power package (at second base, no less), and as with Ripken added Gold Glove defense to the mix. Were they the same price I'd like the Ripken card better, but with a 25 percent difference go for the Sandberg. Two other rookie cards already high in price but with plenty of upward potential are Wade Boggs (#498, $37) and Tony Gwynn (#482, $35). Pick 'em. Good set, all told; just behind the '82 in this writer's mind as a great buy. The '83 Traded set marks Darryl Strawberry's first card appearance; at $100 you don't want it today.

’84 Topps is a set on the slide. Two big rookie cards—those of Don Mattingly (#8) and Strawberry (#182) are the key. Both ballplayers have suffered serious mid-career problems, and as a result the long term potential of those cards and this set is in doubt. Second-line or supporting rookie cards are non-existent here. The '84 Traded set is a much better value, even at its current $100. It has hard-to-find rookie cards of Dwight Gooden and Bret Saberhagen, and caught an unusual number of Hall-of-Famers in mid-season trades.

The star card of the '85 set is the Roger Clemens rookie (#181, $22). Clemens is clearly the most dominant starting pitcher in today's game, and puts up Cy Young-contending numbers season after season. The rest of the set is forgettable, including an overrated subset of U.S. Olympic cards led by Mark McGuire. You don't want the set; you want the Clemens card for sure, and possibly the Kirby Puckett (#536,#18) and Dwight Gooden (#620, $7) rookies. Neither is as safe a bet as Clemens. Neither comes close. The '85 Topps Traded set is dirt-cheap at $25, but unless you're a Vince Coleman fan, you don't want that either.

Topps sets from 1986-89 have all slid in price in recent years, as the crush of cards that Topps printed from '86 on has worked its way into the market. The half-black-bordered '86 set is the most expensive of these at $35, but the much better buy is the '87 set at $27 (and sliding even lower). The '87 set has rookie cards for many of the game's brightest stars, including Will Clark, Jose Canseco, Barry Bonds, Ruben Sierra and many more. Many of the same names can be found on first Topps appearances in the '86 Traded Set, another good buy at the $25 level. The '88 Traded set is the best of the rest, even if currently overpriced at $30. Containing first cards of Jim Abbott, Roberto Alomar, Robin Ventura and many more, it holds the best of the late '80s crop in a single 132-card box.

Fleer

Fleer's initial 1981 offering is worth owning only as a curiosity item. (Of course, if I were curious enough, I'd look at someone else's.) At $50 the price is reasonable, but the poor card quality combines with a typical first-set lack of rookies to make this only a middlin' buy. One note is that the set does hold two Rickey Henderson cards, the second honoring Rickey's single-season stolen base mark. Lots of tribute cards here, for late-career HOFers like Steve Carlton and Reggie Jackson.

Among other things, the '82 Fleer set presents the worst photography on a major set in the modern age. Blurry, off-center shots are the norm, and the basic design added nothing to the overall effect. The set's $85 price tag is almost entirely because of the Ripken, Jr., rookie (#176, $50). There are also two variations of this set's Lee Smith rookie (#603A-B) at about $4 each. Any are okay investments, but the poor card quality makes the Topps or Donruss issues preferable.

The '83 Fleer set offered a marked improvement in appearance, as well debuting what became a distinct Fleer "look." These are clean, bold cards, and from 1983 on Fleer is much more popular with collectors and investors alike. Sandberg, Boggs and Gwynn are present in the '83 set; as individual buys they offer no special advantages or disadvantages versus the other brands.

The '84 set was a relatively scarce issue that rides, as with the other '84 sets, on the two big rookie cards of Mattingly and Strawberry. No single cards from this set reach the "must-own" level, but at $225 the entire set is an item that might yet climb higher. Fleer started to mimic Topps "Traded" set approach with the issue of its own year-end update set in 1984, and the '84 Fleer Update set— at $675—is the most expensive major issue of the decade. It weds extreme scarcity to desirable first cards of four of the decade's better players—Clemens, Puckett, Gooden and Saberhagen. While the set is indeed sought after by wealthier collectors, its already-high price leaves it little room for further growth.

1985 Fleer offers the traditional "rookie" cards for the players mentioned above, and its $175 price tag again reflects its relative scarcity compared to Topps. Neither brand was as hard to find in these years as Donruss, which of course explains why Donruss prices for these sets have climbed so high. We'll get to those Donruss sets soon enough. Other than for its general attractiveness the Fleer set offers nothing that you can't find elsewhere. I've seen this rated as a "four-star" investment value in magazines, but I disagree: it offers nothing more than an alternative to other sets. The '85 Update set, like the Topps one, is a dud. Oddibe McDowell sure looked like he'd be a great ballplayer. He wasn't. Still, this one is scarce enough that $25 to 30, squirreling away one or two of these small boxes might not be a bad idea.

The '86 Fleer cards look much like the '85s; as a set this has slid back from higher levels to its current $125 mark. Over half of that value is due to the two big rookie cards (as today's hobby sees them) of Jose Canseco and Cecil Fielder. Canseco is a superstar battling through an injury-filled period, while Fielder is only another in a long line of Don Baylor/George Bell types, sluggers with high peaks but shorter-than-you-might-think careers. The Canseco card (#649, $40) is becoming a better buy all the time, but the lack of supporting rookies in this issue makes the entire set a questionable purchase at best. The '86 Update set stands roughly equal to the Topps issue, a good buy today at $30 with a number of sure-to-climb rookie cards inside.

1987 Fleer was, for a change, the rarest of the three major brands. Like the other '87 sets it's stuffed with rookies, but is high enough compared to the competition that it won't climb significantly in the near future. At $90 it's a safer bet only over the long haul. '88 Fleer is more common and less desirable than its $36 price tag indicates, and '89 Fleer has dropped dramatically from its mania-driven (the Ripken error craze) highs. The first Fleer appearance of Ken Griffey, Jr., (1989 #548, $9) offers a reasonably-priced alternative to the very expensive Upper Deck Junior issue, while still being much more scarce than the Donruss Griffey rookie.

Donruss

Donruss, like Fleer, issued lots of cards its first two years, made somewhat less through the middle '80s, then turned on the tree-chewers full bore toward the end of the decade. The '81 set, Donruss's first, contains Reardon and Raines rookies and isn't a bad buy today at $55. As with most sets of this era it has many cards showing aging Hall-of-Famers, and as a result will be of interest to many collectors for years to come. Not a blue chip investment, but a good one.

Donruss's 1982 set is a notch rarer, a notch more expensive, and a notch uglier to look at. It's an unattractive set of too-white cards that owes more than half its current worth ($80), like the Fleer set, to its Ripken rookie (#405, $50), and despite the reasonably friendly price tag is not currently much in demand. It does have a neat card of Ted Giannolus, the San Diego Chicken (#531, two varieties at $1 each). At least I think that's Ted inside the costume; rumors circulated that much like the many people working as Ronald McDonalds, there were several Chicken costume-fillers to meet special engagement requests. Only da Chicken knows for sure, but after some battles with his sponsoring radio station da Boid faded from the media glare.

The design of '83 Donruss is almost a mirror image of the 82s. The logo moved from right to left, the name-bearing bat silhouette switched directions, and the white ball was replaced with a brown glove and moved from left to right. Other than that, same card. At $125, this set is a neat match to the Fleer issue, but due to its handsome design the Fleer set is a better buy.

The '84 Donruss set was hard to find, and the result of that can be seen today in its $360 price. The Strawberry and Mattingly rookies present to each '84 set are here as well, and it was the '84 Donruss Mattingly card (#248, $65 today) that rested at the core of the New York-based rookie card rush. That card was once a $100 item; too much it seems for even a great ballplayer with a questionable back. There are no "best bets" from this set—it's an all or nothing deal. If you believe that the set has value, buy the whole thing at once. A blue chip item, but with a price to match.

Yet if '84 Donruss is blue-chip, than '85 Donruss is double blue at half the price ($180). The better rookie mix here makes this one a much stronger long-term buy, with all of the prominent '85 rookies mentioned earlier. My belief is that this set will someday exceed the '84 set in value. The Roger Clemens card at $40 (#273) is a fine choice for the future, and make sure to hold out for one in a true mint grade because minor damage to these black-bordered beauties is easily seen and subtracts big chunks from the card's price.

The '86 Donruss, like the Fleer set, hinges on a single key card—the Jose Canseco rookie (a "Rated Rookie", actually, #39, $75). This is down from a high of $100, and as might be apparent from that, the '86 Canseco was another card that had its day as "the card that everyone just **had** to have." Maybe that day will come again, but in the meantime there's only that card and two other rookie issues to support this set's $165 price. One of those is Cecil Fielder (#512, $25), who's an overrated card investment no matter which brand name you choose. The other rookie here is Fred McGriff (#28, $20), and this card could yet turn out to be the key card of the set. Beyond that there's precious little to be interested in. Donruss also joined Topps and Fleer in issuing a late-season trade/rookie set, and this first Donruss "Rookies" set is the rarest of those for the year. Also the best, and at $60 it holds every major rookie the year produced.

By 1987 Donruss was well aware of the increased demand for cards, and to this day enough of the '87 cards circulate to ensure that the price will remain stable. It's much rarer than Topps but really not rare at all. Still, its current $60 price represents the bottom of a long, slow slide, and better days for this issue lie ahead. It has all the rookies from the great '86-87 crop, and as one of those dastardly black-bordered sets, true "mint" sets and singles will someday be worth extra. The '87 Donruss Rookies set is okay at $20, combining relative rarity with the first card appearance of Matt Williams. Face it: Williams takes a lousy picture, and all Williams cards are unattractive because of it. Is that why they don't sell? Maybe, but Williams cards are better buys than many others.

And if they had the lumberman working overtime in '87, they had them hooked up to an IV full of liquid Vivarin in '88 and '89. "Who needs a chain saw? Teeth work fine." These two sets are everywhere in enormous quantities, and their cheap card quality—the thinnest major-set cards ever produced—meant that Leaf, Inc., got even more of them out of a ton of pulp. They're attractive cards, however, and every collector should own a set. At current prices ($15 each) it's an easy enough thing to manage. Just don't expect them to be worth anything more than that later on.

Score

The fourth entry in the baseball card market made its debut in 1988 with a colorful-yet-somehow-bland set that collectors cooled to later on. Most companies have trouble getting large "rookie" crops into their premier sets, and in 1988 there weren't many rookies debuting anyhow, after the large turnover within the game the two previous years. It's a $15 set today, with no cards within it being necessary to a good collection. The "Traded" set that Score issued later that season, though, is another matter. Same design but far more scarce, and today the hobby recognizes this scarcity and has fixed this tough box with a neat $60 price. A potentially great rookie card in Roberto Alomar leads the way, with enough support from rookie appearances of Grace, McDowell and others to suggest that this set may climb much higher.

Both '89 Score issues are forgettable, except to collectors who just happen to like Score. The regular set is $15, the traded set $10, so they're within almost every buyer's range. Don't worry about the rookies. There just aren't that many here.

Upper Deck

Which bring us to Upper Deck, which burst on the scene in mid-1989 with a large 700-card issue featuring stylish design and sharp, game-action photos. Later came a 100-card update set, making the whole issue a continuous 800-card run, and today complete sets already top the $200 plateau. The set's key card has turned out to be the rookie card of Ken Griffey, Jr., (#1, $65) another one of those must-own cards that seems to continually spiral upward. It's a desirable card, and many more hot young names clutter the set. What makes this set such a great investment is that it was the single issue that transformed the card market: the introduction of premium-grade cards began here, and the hobby recognizes it and accords this set extra worth because of it. In terms of price versus scarcity, this set is already out of proportion. In terms of price versus demand, however, the balance may still be tipped the other way.

FOOTBALL
Topps

The explosion that began in the baseball card market in 1985 or 1986 took a while longer to reach football. Topps had the market to itself until 1989, when both Score and Pro Set, a Texas-based trading card company, issued new products. Also making a minor market debut was the brand new name of Action Packed, with a tiny 30-card set bringing up-scale cards to the football market for the first time.

The 1980 Topps set is one of the weaker sets of the decade in terms of rookie cards in which to invest. The most expensive card in the set is the first issue for Giants' quarterback Phil Simms (#225, $18), and the second costliest is the Ottis Anderson rookie (#170, $10). Neither is a good purchase; both rank as long shots to make the Pro Football Hall of Fame. Despite that, there are some interesting cards here, and the set as a whole (for about $75) is a balanced issue that merits strong consideration. Best bets here are second-year cards for Ozzie Newsome (#110, $5.50) and James Lofton (#78, $8).

The '81 Topps set is currently the most expensive set of the decade, with its $225 tag spearheaded by rookie cards of Joe Montana (#216, $150) and Art Monk (#194, $45). Both cards are worth owning but neither is an appetizing buy at present levels; they're risk-free, but can't climb as rapidly as they have in the past few years. A comparative steal from the set is the rookie issue for tight end Kellen Winslow (#150, $7). Winslow was the major star on the other end of San Diego's "Air Fouts" offense, and is due to receive much more recognition than this card's current price would indicate.

The '82 set goes for less than half the price of the '81, at $100, and while the sure bet here is the Lawrence Taylor rookie card (#434, $28), the better investment is the Anthony Munoz rookie (#51) at $9. You mean **really?** Actually buy a card of a (gasp!

choke!) **offensive tackle?** Well, sure, especially when the tackle in question has been recognized for years as the best lineman in the game. He may not throw touchdown passes, but Canton will nonetheless someday house a Munoz plaque. Not quite as great an investment as the Taylor card is the Ronnie Lott rookie (#486, $28); Lott's years as the defensive leader for the championship 49ers make his Hall election an almost certain bet. Toss in the second-year Montana card and this set is one of the better bargains around.

The '83 set is even more affordable, at $60, yet offers only one rookie card astute investors should want, that of Chicago middle linebacker Mike Singletary (#38, $10). Forget about the more expensive Marcus Allen card (#294, $11); the Singletary card is the one to own.

The '84 Topps set climbs back up the ol' price ladder. This recently popular set now carries a $100 price, and as you might have guessed, it's another quarterback rookie card that leads the way. In this case it's Dan Marino (#123, $48), supported by first appearances by John Elway (#63, $17), Eric Dickerson (#280, $15), Roger Craig (#353, $7) and Darrell Green (#380, $6). Wise buyers might snap the Green card from that batch before anything else, but the true bargain of the batch is the first card for Saints' placekicker Morten Andersen (#300), an absolute steal at $1.50. Now that placekickers have broken the ice at the HOF, a few of the best will be recognized. Andersen was the best kicker of the '80s.

1984 also saw Topps issue a much rarer set picturing players in the upstart United States Football League (USFL). Topp's USFL cards lasted exactly as long as the league did, that is to say, two years. In an attempt to garner fan support and a lucrative TV contract, the USFL signed several of the biggest new names. That and the scarcity of the cards explains this set's $400 price. The most expensive card is Jim Kelly (#36, $190), followed by Herschel Walker (#74, $72), Reggie White (#58, $48), and Steve Young (#52, $38). Even Scott Norwood costs $4, and Chuck Fusina—remember Chuck Fusina?—goes a buck. For the future, the White card is the best bet of the batch, but if you're watching this set with a loving eye, you've got too much money.

The '85 Topps. An overpriced set at $80. Warren Moon is a fine quarterback but started too late to put up those awesome career statistics investors like, and his first issue (#251, $33) has little backing here from other cards. The '85 USFL set that Topps put out while the league itself struggled for survival is costlier at $125 and is in the same league as an investment: you don't need it.

Topps in '86 issued a set of ugly cards with green-and-white candy-cane-striped borders. Come to think of it, none of the '80s sets represent new levels of esthetic achievement, but when you're the only kid in the sandbox, what does it matter? The '86 set today costs $90 and is recommended strongly at that price. It is spearheaded by its Jerry Rice rookie card (#161, $45), perhaps the most buyable $45 '80s-vintage card in the hobby today. Rice's utter statistical domination of the game's receiving corps is well-known but still obscured by Montana's shadow. When the dust settles, however, the talent that Jerry Rice was will get full due. A first card for Al Toon (#101, $6) offers long-shot possibilities, while the first NFL card for Reggie White (#275, $5) is a safe bet.

'87 Topps is more affordable at $50, but also more common. Quarterbacks Jim Kelly and Randall Cunningham have rookie cards here. Kelly, though, had the previous USFL issues, and the Cunningham card (#296, $14) ranks as a riskier but better buy, if only because large numbers of the Cunningham card suffer from a plate flaw that during printing left black streaks in the card's picture.

The '88 Topps set is even more common than the '87s, as the expansion of the football card market—two years or so delayed from that in baseball—began in earnest. The '88 set is a cheap enough buy today at $24, but only the first card of Neal Anderson (#71, $4) merits attention. Easy to ignore are cards of Bo Jackson and Christian Okoye. Second-best bet is the Cornelius Bennett rookie (#230, $1.75).

The last Topps set of the decade, the '89s, is a common-as-dirt issue with only one rookie, Thurman Thomas, now worth mentioning. It's cheap enough at $12-14, and even cheaper is the first football Traded set at $7. The '89 Topps Traded is the better buy of the two, led by its Barry Sanders card (#83T, $4). Both '89 Topps issues are too common to climb much in the next few years.

Score

The arrival of the competition occurred in 1989 as well, meaning that football cards were everywhere for the first time. Score's first football issue was a stiff on the store shelves but turned out to be scarce. Recent speculation has driven this set all the way to $180, and with rookie appearances by all of the season's new names it stands today as the '89 set collectors wish to own. The Sanders rookie in this set (#257) already fetches $50, and is supported by Thomas and the overrated Troy Aikman. It's also a rookie quarterback bonanza, with Mark Rypien, Chris Miller, and even Don Majkowski, but today's best buy from the set is probably the Keith Jackson rookie card (#101) at $4. Score followed this regular issue with a late-season supplemental set, and while $22 add-on offers only a Sterling Sharpe rookie card (#3335, $4) as a buy for the future, unless one of the rookie linemen here surges from the pack as Munoz did several years before.

Pro Set

And then came Pro Set, which hit the market with an advertising blitz that ensured this new football product would garner solid sales. Good thing, too, because Pro Set cards were made in large quantities, and as that became evident to the hobby the price for this set slid back some from its early highs. Today the set holds steady at $30, with rookie cards of Sanders and the rest that are less common than Topps's versions but far more available than Score's. Pro Set also printed tons of a "Final Edition" update set, which can be yours today for $3 or as a premium for buying eight gallons of gas at your local MotoMart. Okay, six gallons. Two sets. Six. Whatever—it's a cheapie.

Action Packed

The '89 Action Packed set was really only a test version of a product that made a full-blown appearance in '90. It's an '89 set, though, so it's mentioned here. These computer-edited, raised-surface cards came only four to a pack, so that completing a 30-card set was at least a little tougher than it sounds. The most expensive singles from this set aren't great buys **as singles,** but as a $25 set this limited issue will always have potential to climb.

BASKETBALL

Topps

Topps basketball cards were steady but disappointing sellers throughout the '70s, and after the '81-82 season they pulled the plug on the sport. Even the renewed interest in basketball cards at the end of the decade has failed to yank Topps back into this market, although several other companies were happy to fill the hole.

The '79-80 Topps basketball set is a colorful 132-card issue that ranks as one of Topps's better basketball efforts of the era. The cards were standard-sized, unlike earlier jumbo efforts, and while this $80 set is sparse on rookies (Alex English being the biggest name), it is scarce enough and has enough big name cards within it to be worth the cost. Cards of players like Kareem Abdul-Jabbar, Julius Erving and Rick Barry will always hold their value, and the Barry card (#120, $3.50) might be the best choice of the batch.

The '80-81 Topps set is unusual and entertaining at best, obnoxious at worst. Actually, these are a lot of fun, even if they're some of the strangest basketball "cards" ever made. Each normal-sized card is in fact made up of three side-by-side "mini" cards with perforations between, and since the cards were printed on two different sheets, much player repetition exists. All told, the set is complete at 176, each holding a unique three-mini-card combination. Separated individuals are worth far less than the three-player cards from which they came. The complete set brings a hefty $450, due almost entirely to the first card appearances of Magic Johnson and Larry Bird, the two biggest stars of the decade. While both the Bird and Johnson card thirds exist on several complete cards, the key card (#6, $250) sandwiches the pair around a Julius Earving team-leader shot. Have a favorite player? You'll find several of him in this strange set.

The '81-82 season brought the final Topps entry, a nationally-distributed 66-card series paired with three regionally-distributed (East, Midwest, West) high-number runs. Complete sets run about $90, and even though the second-year Bird and

Magic cards outshine a weak rookie crop, the scarcity of the set makes this one a better-than-average investment.

Star Co.

From 1983 to 1986 there were no **major** makers of basketball cards. The closest things were the '83-84 through '85-86 Star Co. sets, which were distributed as team sets but were collectively numbered and can be combined into a set as a whole. None of these sets are common, and the rarest varieties, such as the '83-84 Dallas Mavericks, may exist in quantities as small as 500 of each card. Prices for the scarcest team sets approach $1,000, and complete sets go $1,500-3,000.

Fleer

Fleer took over the basketball card reins during the '86-87 season with the issuance of a 132-card set that ranks as one of the most popular and important sets of the decade. It is an incredible set in terms of rookies, led by Michael Jordan (#57, $325), Patrick Ewing (#32, $90), Karl Malone (#68, $60), and cards of Charles Barkley, Clyde Drexler, Isiah Thomas, Akeem Olajuwon, Chris Mullin, Dominique Wilkins and Tom Chambers right behind. Containing arguably the best Hall of Fame "rookie" crop ever, this set is unfortunately already beyond the reach of most collectors' budgets with its $750 tag. A great set, and one that will hold its value for as long as there is interest in cards.

The next year's set ('87-88) is a pale cousin by comparison, but the few rookies here like Chuck Person and Terry Porter are more than ably supported by the second-year cards of all the players listed above. This set is more affordable at $235, yet doesn't have the ceiling-busting potential of the '86-87s. The '88-89 set is even less costly ($85), and with rookies including Scottie Pippen, Reggie Miller and Dennis Rodman, this one is a better bet than the previous year. The '89-90 set continues the descent into the land of more common, more affordable buys, and yet the deep but lukewarm rookie batch here (led by Kevin Johnson) makes this one only a so-so bet.

Hoops

Making its debut in the '89-90 season, this Impel Marketing set soon captured a chunk of the basketball market. Later over-printing of the Hoops cards led to a general apathy toward the brand, but the first Hoops set (300 cards, $65) stands as a decent buy. The reason for the $65 cost is the rookie-card appearance of one-time Navy standout David Robinson (#138, $38). Robinson may be a basketball version of Darryl Strawberry, never quite being able to live up to the enormous expectations the basketball world had, but if you like the Robinson card enough to invest in it, just go ahead and buy the whole set. Sets were notoriously difficult to assemble from boxes and packs and didn't come in a "factory set" variety, and as a whole this issue has room for growth.

The late-season addition of 52 more Hoops cards brought the total for the year to 352. The update series costs $12.50, with $9 of that coming from a second Robinson card. The same rule applies to this one: buy the whole set at once, even if you're buying it only for the Robinson card.

HOCKEY

While the Topps and O-Pee-Chee sets (the Canadian company licensed to make hockey cards) were and are separate entities, for purposes of this brief summary the two brands will be considered as one. Topps hockey cards were not always available through the '80s; for the '82-83 and '83-84 seasons, O-Pee-Chee was the only available brand. But O-Pee-Chee and Topps cards use the same design and (for the most part) picture the same players, and are generally considered to be two versions of the same product. The O-Pee-Chee sets are much larger, reflecting the greater Canadian interest in the sport, yet the major players normally appear in both sets. Unless otherwise mentioned, the cards referred to here are the Topps (American) versions, although for the two Topps-less seasons the O-Pee-Chee sets will be detailed.

The '79-80 Topps set stands as one of the great hockey sets, as its $600 price suggests. The key here is the rookie card for Wayne Gretzky (#18, $400) and the enormous cost of that single card exactly represents the impact Gretzky had on the sport of hockey. Even though hockey sports a grand tradition, it was

Gretzky who helped make the sport important to much of America, especially the West Coast. But though this is the "Gretzky" set, it has more to offer: the last card appearances of Gordie Howe (#175, $25) and Bobby Hull (#185, $17.50). A classic.

The key card from the '80-81 Topps set would be the rookie appearance of Ray Bourque (#140, $60), if not for being overshadowed by the Gretzky phenomenon. No less than six cards feature Gretzky in one form or another, and what is considered his true second-year card (#250, $150) ranks as the most expensive card of the set. Almost forgotten behind Gretzky and Bourque are the first appearances of Mike Liut (#31, $3) and Brian Propp (#39, $5), two of several cards worthy of individual attention.

The regional distribution Topps tried with its basketball set was repeated with the '81-82 hockey issue. The first 66 cards were issued nationally, and second and third 66-card series were split between "East" and "West" distributions. $95 brings home all 198 cards, and at that it's one of the decade's better values. This Gretzky-supported set holds strong rookie cards of Jari Kurri and Peter Stastny, and the "West" subset has harder-to-find cards of Dino Ciccarelli and Denis Savard.

('82-83 O-Pee-Chee): Boasting yet another flood of Gretzky cards, including the all-important "Shorthanded Goal Leader" card. An okay buy for the hockey fanatic at $125, and also containing a decent rookie crop with Grant Fuhr, Dale Hawerchuk and Joe Mullen, among others.

('83-84 O-Pee-Chee): Same price as the '82-83 OPCs; roughly the same set. Lots of Gretzky cards and an okay rookie crop, including Steve Larmer, Bernie Nicholls, Mats Naslund and the tragedy-stricken Pelle Lindbergh.

The '84-85 season marked the return of Topps hockey cards to the American marketplace, and this $45 set is keyed by the rookie card of Steve Yzerman (#49, $12.50). It's an affordable buy at that price, and for the money spent, a worthwhile one.

The second biggest rookie card of the decade makes its appearance in the '85-86 set. The player pictured, of course, was Mario Lemieux, and this first Lemieux card (#9, $110) has carried this set all the way up to its current $165 mark. The second-line rookies here are okay but nothing spectacular; people in a betting mood could play the Kelly Hrudey/Tomas Sandstrom/Pat LaFon-taine trifecta and come up big. Or maybe not, but this is the "Le-mieux" set, and always will be.

The strength of Lemieux's appeal makes his second-year card currently the most valuable item ($35) in the '86-87 set, but a bet-ter buy for the long term is the first issue for Hall-bound goalie Pa-trick Roy (#53, $25). Folks interested in a riskier card with greater profit potential should check out the Petr Klima rookie (#98), cur-rently costing only $4. As a whole, this set is average. Better than some, worse than others, and with a middlin' price tag to match.

The '87-88 Topps set stands as today as a better buy, given that its current price is roughly the same at $110. A deeper rookie crop is the difference, with several players here having decent Hall potential. Luc Robitaille might lead the list, but also considered by hockey card investors are cards of Adam Oates, Rick Tocchet, Esa Tikkanen and Ron Hextall. The Hextall card (#169, $3.75) is as at-tractive as any, for the price.

Not yet affected by the surge in cards being issued for other sports, the '88-89 Topps set still boasts relative rarity as a major component of its $126 price. The Brett Hull rookie card (#66, $60) is the key here and the third great rookie card of the decade, but people unfamiliar with this set should know that the Hull card was one of several that was "double-printed." Double-printing means that the Hull card, among several, was printed on two different sheets that were cut into cards for the final mix. Since all sheets are printed in equal quantities, this means that there are twice as many Hull cards to go around. The set is not recommended as a great buy at this time, if only because of uncertainty about the double-printed card.

Finishing up the list is the '89-90 Topps set. Printed in much greater numbers than all the earlier sets, this one nonetheless has enough variety to support a $35 price. The second-year Hull card (#186, $8.50) rivals the Joe Sakic rookie (#113, $10) as the set's most expensive card, but a better bet than either could be Brian Leetch (#136, $3). Or perhaps not; given that the players debuting in these later sets have played only one fourth to one third of their careers, these last choices slide deep into the land of speculation.

So far the 1990s may be considered a continuation of the 1980s as trends begun in the late 1980s continue. The explosion of interest in cards and in numbers of cards continues at a pace worthy of a chain reaction.

It has been suggested that there were more different football cards produced in one year in the 1990s than in all previous years combined. That observation probably applies to basketball and perhaps hockey. It certainly applies to all other sports except boxing and baseball.

It has not been merely types of cards either. Production levels have also risen for regular issues as companies seek not an orderly market, but rather impressive profits for their stockholders. Add to those quantities new "limited edition" high priced, high quality sets and sets for any market real, imagined, or potential and you get the picture-a world awash in cardboard.

Were everything normal as in ancient times such as 1986, it would still be too early to pick out potentially promising cards from the sets of the 1990s. Sure, Jeff George may have potential as a quarterback and Tim Hardaway as a point guard, but two years in any sport is too early to draw sound conclusions.

If you want cards from the 1990s right now you want them either because you collect them or because you are speculating, not because you are investing either in the card or in the player. That's because in both cases, it's too early to draw any conclusions.

Bo Jackson looked good until the injury. Good as he was in both baseball and football the chances are he's not going to be in either Hall of Fame and his card will be priced only slightly above a common some day. Wally Berger hit 38 home runs as a rookie but is priced only slightly above a common (if that) today. The list is endless in all sports. The message is simply that one or two seasons do not a career make.

In the '90s it's even worse. Virtually every card company would have you believe that a "limited edition" sold naturally at a higher price is a better investment due to their smaller number of cards. It makes sense if prices were based solely on rarity but they aren't. You could contend that T213s made only in Louisiana were "limited editions" of T206s. Are they priced at multiples of T206s to reflect their many times greater rarity? Certainly not, because only a handful of people care, so despite greater rarity their prices are very similar to T206s.

Almost from the time of the first card there have been so-called premium sets. In early times they were bigger cabinet cards which were also produced in far smaller quantities than regular issues yet there is no conclusive proof or even strong evidence that such premium cards are better investments, meaning the limited edition premium card of today is also speculation as an investment even if you pick the right players.

In a few years we will begin to get an idea of what cards of the '90s represent the real investments. Until then collect at will and speculate at your own peril.

Buyer Beware

Not every investment that the people who sell sports cards and memorabilia claim is a great investment is a great investment. Like any other sort of money-making proposition, sports-memorabilia investibles come in all grades, from AAA to junk. If you buy junk, sometimes you'll score huge returns and sometimes you'll be left with . . . cardboard. The upside to that: If the cardboard goes bad at least you can stick it in the spokes of your bicycle. The down side: If the cardboard goes really bad you may be riding your bicycle a lot more than you'd like. This chapter takes a look at a wide range of sports-memorabilia investibles, from autographed balls to holograms, from the standpoint of, "What could possibly go wrong with these?" Call it "An Investor's Guide To Staying On the Safe Side."

ROOKIE CARDS

Rookie cards are the penny stocks of the sports-memorabilia market, for all that entails: quick profits and equally rapid declines. But the spectacularity of the rookie-card market has been sorely overstated.

Here's how it's supposed to work: You buy cards of a certain rookie at 10 cents, and sell them when the rookie does well and his card sells for $7.

That's how it's supposed to work—and the fact that it often does actually work that way is astounding in and of itself. But for it to work that way, you have to hit quite a few variables squarely on the head.

First, you have to pick the right rookie to buy. Ideally, you want a player who is not regarded highly at this point but who stands a very good chance of moving into the starting lineup and producing in headline-grabbing fashion. This rules out utility infielders, tough-checking wingers, slap-hitting outfielders, offensive linemen, rugged rebounding forwards, relief pitchers, punters, starting pitchers who don't strike out many batters, catchers, defensemen and all but the fastest base stealers. This includes power hitters, quarterbacks, wide receivers, high-scoring guards and forwards, top goalies, quarterback-sacking defensive linemen and linebackers, goal-scoring centericemen and wingers, and hard-throwing starting pitchers.

How do you find young players who fit this ideal? For all sports except baseball, follow the colleges as closely as you can. For hockey, read *Hockey News;* in baseball, read *Baseball America.* It's a publication for and about the minor leagues, published every two weeks, give or take. No other periodical gives you the sort of information on the minors you get in *BA.* Lots of other baseball-card investors read *BA,* too, so you're not likely to score any big gains if you pick who they pick. Instead, analyze minor-league statistics, looking for strikeout-to-innings-pitched ratios for pitchers and home-runs-to-at-bats ratios for hitters. These are the key numbers, in addition to the normal batting-average/won-lost-record figures. Don't rely on one season's stats, either, since minor-league stats can change pretty radically as players move from organization to organization, level to level and park to park. Track minor-leaguers; look for improvement in numbers as a player moves up through the system. That, as much as anything, will tip you off to future minor-leaguers.

Okay, assuming you've picked the right players, then you have to pick the right card. This used to be easy, but isn't anymore.

Before you had to deal only with the regular set of cards from each of three or four or five manufacturers, and then their end-of-year update/traded set. If the player wasn't in the regular set, chances would be very good that he would be in the traded set if he played at all that year. Whatever the case, you just went for his first card, bought it and stood pat. Today, all those sets are in place, but so are mid-year sets, end-of-end-of-year sets, sets in series, ancillary sets, pre-rookie sets (more on those later), mid-range sets, high-end sets, ultra-high-end sets, and low-end sets. It's no longer a matter of picking the first card of a player; today you have to pick the first card of a player *that everyone is subsequently going to want*. Holy swami, Batman. It's like picking a hit movie before it's a hit or a hot stock before it's hot; if you could do that all the time you wouldn't have to work.

Take Frank Thomas. His first cards are in the 1990 Score and Topps sets. But no one by comparison wants those. They all want the 1990 Leaf card of Thomas, which wasn't his first card by a long shot, came out at the end of the season, and had nothing going for it but a high level of perceived scarcity. That was enough; the '90 Leaf Thomas is, for all intents and purposes, his rookie card, all logic to the contrary.

What can you do? When you evaluate a rookie card as an investible, project the future performance of the set as well as the future performance of the player. If you feel you don't know enough about the market to do that, buy a player's first Upper Deck cards, if you can. The company has a reputation—deserved or not—for making high-quality, low-print-run sets, and makes about as liquid a card as you can find. Topps is the common denominator of cards; you can find them everywhere, but because you can find them everywhere, few people want to sink investment dollars in them. Some with Score and Pro Set (in football and hockey) and Hoops (in basketball), though these companies make a much higher quality card than Topps and their assortment of rookies is usually better than just about anyone's. Donruss and Fleer are trying to position themselves between Score and Upper Deck, but their array of rookies in any given year is likely to be mediocre. The high-end cards—Leaf, Studio, Topps Stadium Club, Fleer Ultra and Score Pinnacle, Parkhurst, Pro Set Platinum, Action Packed,

O-Pee-Chee Premier, Collector's Edge, and who-knows-what-else in football—take turns being hot or also-rans. Their selections of rookies can vary widely.

Here's another source for you to consider: *Baseball Cards* magazine rates the top 100 baseball rookie cards for that given year in its April issue. It takes into account a player's past-season performance, his projected future performance, the current price of a card and its appreciation potential and ranks them all on 10-point scales to determine the year's best rookie cards. The system works; 1992's top rookie was Cleveland third baseman Jim Thome, but Minnesota's Pat Mahomes and Baltimore's Mike Mussina—two of the year's hottest rookies and leading contenders for the American League Rookie of the Year award—were rated surprisingly highly, and recommended as "best buys." Past years have tipped people off to John Kruk, Mike Greenwell, Marquis Grissom, Ruben Sierra, Barry Larkin, Roberto Alomar, and Mark McGwire.

There's also the question of how many cards of each player to buy. That's largely a function of how expensive each card is and how much you want to spend. My rule of thumb on spending is: The less expensive a card is, the more of that card you should buy. As a rule, stay away from any rookie card that comes out of the chute priced at 75 cents and above, simply because of the difficulty you'll have making good money on the card. It's infinitely more difficult for a $1.25 card to go to $2.50 than it is for a 50-cent card to go to $1, or a quarter card to 50 cents. There's no reason you can't buy some $1.25 cards if you feel absolutely sure that player can make it up to $2.50, but you should buy fewer of these cards and balance them with plenty of 25-centers.

With cards in the nickel-to-25-cent price range, buy from 500 to 1,000 of each player. If you feel you've found a can't-miss player you can (and should) buy more, but only if that purchase is tempered with buys of other cards that will enable you to trim your losses if need be.

The last major question to be answered is when to buy. Two times are best: At the very start of the card season, and in the case of players who don't perform up to expectations, one year to 18 months after that. The best prices for all players' cards can be found very early on, before the pre-season hype gets too great. However, if a hyped baseball or hockey player doesn't perform up to expectations or is sent down to the minors—a common occurrence, as card sets are filled more and more with players who are a year or two away from sticking in the big leagues—prices can fall and cards can actually be cheaper than they were the previous fall. It's a dangerous strategy if you're betting on specific players to fall, but if you just want to go through and cherrypick off-year rookies, it works extremely well.

Here's an example of how well this sort of strategy can work —when it works.

An acquaintance called me up one day in 1989 and asked me about Delino DeShields. I told him I thought he had the potential at that point in his career (he was still in Class-A baseball) to be a very special player and an interesting card buy, seeing as how O-Pee-Chee, Topps' Canadian licensee, had put a card of him and three other Canadian draft picks in its set, and Topps hadn't. He agreed, and began buying Delino DeShields O-Pee-Chee cards wherever he could find them. Before long he had more than 100,000 Delino DeShields cards for an average of 20 cents apiece and had essentially cornered the market in DeShields. He also bought slightly fewer cards of Toronto's top draft pick that year, an outfielder named Derek Bell. My acquaintance then sat and waited, and when DeShields came up to Montreal and began playing well he started selling the cards, for prices ranging from $5 to $10 each. After DeShields cooled, he sold his Derek Bell cards for virtually the same price.

My acquaintance had done everything right: He had done his research, picked the right card, bought it at the right time for the right price, and in this case, because he was so sure of his success, he bought the right amount. And he was rewarded handsomely for his efforts.

Before you think that this guy must be rich as Croesus—or at least Donald Trump—here's the rest of the story: He turned around and sunk a huge chunk of his profits from his DeShields cards into cards of Bob Hamelin, a sorebacked slugger who may never make the majors. It's a crap shoot, a wildcatter's paradise, and sometimes you hit gushers and sometimes you sink holes in sand.

The only other thing you have to consider with rookie cards is when and how to sell. Though you may have to wait two or three years with some rookies, the ideal turnaround time for rookie cards is six to twelve months. The faster you can turn around a card the better. This is one area where you want to keep your money moving.

The actual act of selling may pose a problem. Unless you live in an area where a hot rookie plays, or a rookie is so hot that he's hot nationwide, you may have trouble selling 1,500 Dean Palmer or Harvey Williams cards. You can avoid this by buying cards of local heroes outside of town and then selling them in town, or you can contact dealers who advertise in *Sports Collectors Digest* that they buy current cards. Try to match up the geographical area of your rookies with the geographical area of dealers you want to sell to. And don't be surprised if a dealer offers you a percentage of a card's book value. That's just the way it is in this business. A dealer is rarely going to offer you full book, no matter how badly he may want a card of yours. If you have a dealer who you buy quite a bit from and have a good relationship with, you might ask him to monitor buy ads on the sports-card teletype services and look for someone wanting to buy your cards. You'll get the best prices on the teletype because it runs on hype, and if you have the hot guy of the moment you can really cash in.

ERROR CARDS

Hardly a day goes by without the editors of the nation's sports-collecting periodicals getting a call: "Yeah, I got one of these cards of Keith Comstock that says he's with the Cubs but he's got a Mariners uniform on, and I know for a fact that he never played for the Mariners, so this card ought to be worth an awful lot of money—right?"

The editors of the nation's sports-collecting periodicals hate to break his heart, but they do.

Error cards, as a rule, just aren't worth very much money, and most make lousy investments. Let's repeat that again, for the perception-impaired: ERROR CARDS, AS A RULE, AREN'T WORTH VERY MUCH MONEY, AND THEY MAKE LOUSY IN-VESTMENTS. The problem is the average collector isn't much interested in an error card unless he has it, and feels he can sell it for a lot of money. He doesn't want a card of Dale Murphy batting left-handed; he wants the money for a card of Dale Murphy batting left-handed. So with error cards you basically have a bunch of buyers looking to peddle cards to other buyers who want to peddle cards to other buyers. Few people want to buy these cards to keep them.

If through some quirk of fate you should come across a big-money error card, sell it as soon as you can and move on to something else. The value history for these cards, if you were to graph it, would show a sudden rise, a plateau, and in some cases, a retreat from that plateau. These are not cards that go up and keep going up. There are few exceptions to this rule.

PROMO CARDS

Promo cards are error cards without the errors. They're ostensibly made by card companies to send to dealers and writers to promote an upcoming card set. What they're really meant to do is create a false impression of scarcity that might rub off on the upcoming set, boosting sales for a set that's otherwise as common as dirt, and about as valuable.

If you're a fan of some of the home-shopping cable channels —and who isn't?—you've probably seen these cards thrown in as inducements to buy a $25 item that the show is selling for $40 but claims is a $100 value. How scarce can a card be if a home-shopping network has one to give out to every misguided soul who orders?

Avoid these cards like the plague, even the ones that are truly scarce promotional items. They're not liquid and they're a gim-mick. Their price curve is a steep climb up immediately followed by a steep plunge down—but the curve never gets high enough to make the enterprise worthwhile. Promo cards are duplicitous, nasty things, and I don't like them.

MINOR-LEAGUE CARDS

The whole question of what constitutes a baseball player's rookie card is leading more and more people to minor-league cards, and it shouldn't. Minor-league cards and major-league cards are two totally different entities, what goes in major-league cards might not go in minor-league cards, and vice versa. Up until just the last couple of years, minor-league cards were sold almost exclusively in team sets, and those team sets were never broken up, regardless of the rookie who might be inside. The notion of a pack of minor-league cards was absurd. Now there are packs of minor-league cards, and sometimes the notion is still absurd.

The advantages of minor-league cards to an investor are obvious: Low print runs—often as few as 5,000—and the idea that the card you buy is the very first one of that player. The disadvantages aren't quite as obvious but are just as substantial: poor liquidity, the possibility of counterfeits, and the fact that if you're buying cards of current minor-leaguers right now, it's an absolute crapshoot. Everything that was just said about rookie cards goes quadruple for minor-league cards. Out of a universe of almost 150 teams and 4,500 players you have to find the two or three players who are going to electrify major-league baseball in a year or two, and then you have to find the right set, either a team set or an overall set, that people are going to want four or five years from now.

It's a little easier for investors to buy minor-league cards now that companies are issuing overall minor-league sets. SkyBox International (formerly Impel Marketing, and CMC before that) has a set it calls "Pre-Rookie Cards" (formerly "Line Drive") that covers Double-A and Triple-A players. Classic-Best (formerly Best Cards) has a set full of all the bells and whistles you'd associate with major-league sets—limited-edition signed-and-numbered cards, holograms, gold-foil cards—and players from the Class-A and Double-A levels. Upper Deck has entered the market this year with an all-level minor-league set that promises to be the best set of all, with the best possibility of growth for the investor.

Approach even Upper Deck's minor-league cards with care. Choose the players you wish to invest in carefully. Use *Baseball America*, but better yet, if you can see any of these players in person, do that. When you find dealers who sell singles, make sure the price you pay is low enough that you'll be able to make a decent profit on the transaction. Realize that liquidity is likely to be bad and profits are going to look much more substantial on paper than they will in the flesh. I don't know of many people who have made a killing on minor-league cards—but on the other hand, I don't know of many who have tried. That will change.

DRAFT-PICK SETS

Draft-pick sets are like minor-league cards, only a worse investment. They're popular with card manufacturers who haven't been able to get licenses to do major sets in any sports because they fall into a gray area between the colleges and the pros. A player who's drafted has no eligibility left to lose and isn't yet property of the big club for licensing purposes, so technically he's free game for anyone who wants to negotiate with him, for whatever price they can sign him to. Sometimes those prices are substantial; Desmond Howard, last year's Heisman Trophy winner, signed an exclusive contract with Classic that paid him in excess of $100,000 —just for a set or two that will only be in demand between the time he leaves college and the day he plays his first pro game.

As you might have gathered, draft-pick sets are not the best place to put your money. Print runs are high, and there tend to be few surprises; the cards that cost the most out of the chute tend to be the cards that cost the most at the end of the year. Proliferation of sets in this area has also reduced total demand for these cards and added another layer of confusion to an already confused situation. Draft-pick sets have all the earmarks of a short-term phenomena; they're to be avoided.

CHASE CARDS

The latest craze on the market is "chase cards"—limited-edition cards randomly inserted into packs at a rate of about one card every 100,000 packs. These have included autographed cards of Ted Williams, Joe DiMaggio, Joe Namath, Joe Montana and Mickey Mantle; hologram cards; instant-win cards; "wild" point-value cards; and even 24-karat-gold cards.

These cards turn innocent packs of cards into mini-lotteries where the chances of winning a prize are as distant as Pluto. If you get one in a pack, bully for you; turn around and sell it for cash as quickly as you can. Like error cards, chase cards have a short, fragile lifespan. They are sought-after for the time they're on the market and companies are promoting them and people are finding them and trying to sell them, but after that they tend to go flat. It would be easier for Cecil Fielder to pass through the eye of a needle than it would be for these cards to double in value. And what goes for these goes double for some of the limited-edition, single-star hologram sets you see offered on the home-shopping shows. Single-player sets have never been very popular, and the fact that the cards are holograms hasn't done anything to change that. If it's expensive and out of the mainstream, stay away; no good will come of it.

COUNTERFEIT CARDS

One of the major concerns of card investors—as it should be —is counterfeit cards. They're a real danger to the investor looking to buy big-money cards of recent vintage. Counterfeits are usually made of cards issued in the last ten to fifteen years—Brett Hull, Michael Jordan and Wayne Gretzky cards are favorites—and are improving in quality every day. It's becoming more and more difficult to tell the genuine cards from the fakes, and this situation will get worse, not better, as more and more modern-era cards sell for increasingly large sums.

The only sure way to detect a counterfeit card is to find a copy of the same card *you know is genuine* and compare the two side by side under the highest-power magnification you can find. Look at the way letters are formed, and watch for irregularities or blurred letters. Look at the dot pattern in pictures for irregularities. Examine the paper. Check the type faces front and back. Never buy a big-money card without at the very least taking it out of its holder, holding it up to a bright light, and eyeing it over the best you can. Krause Publications has printed a very helpful *Counterfeit Detection Guide* that lists all known counterfeits and gives tips for detecting them. A loose-leaf version made available to dealers is continually being expanded. Ask your dealer to look at a copy; if he doesn't have one, buy a consumer's copy of the book and carry it with you whenever you go to buy cards.

MEMORABILIA

Many investor dollars are being shifted away from cards to memorabilia. This shifting has been aided by the development of big-money sports auctions around the country conducted by many of the world's top auction houses—Sotheby's, Christie's, Wolfer's—as well as by the notion that cards is cards is cards; memorabilia is unique.

Unfortunately for the investor, there are even more pitfalls in memorabilia investing than there are in card investing. Counterfeits are much more prevalent and harder to detect, and your chances of making money on a given item varies from item to item because everything is—you guessed it—unique.

Autographs are attracting much of the attention right now, and autographs are a long-standing collectible/investible field. The ground rules for buying autographs are: Single-signed baseballs are the preferred medium; stuff with stories to back it up is usually genuine; Lou Gehrig and Babe Ruth are super-hot; anything outside of baseball isn't doing much now; and dead guys are best overall.

When it comes to detecting counterfeits, you're going to be more helpless than you were trying to detect counterfeit cards. Buy a copy of Krause Publications' *Baseball Autograph Handbook*. It shows you what makes a genuine signature and describes known fakes, in addition to giving you lots of other tips on buying and selling autographs.

If you purchase autographed items at an auction with an eye towards reselling the item, don't get caught in auction hype and pay too much; remember, there's often a 10 percent buyer's premium attached to the sale of an item. Also, because Lou Gehrig and Babe Ruth are super-hot, their autographs should be avoided unless you can pick them up very cheaply. The prices most of their items sell for now are unrealistic, from a money-making standpoint.

The second tip—buy stuff with stories—is just another way of saying, "Get verification." If the item comes with a letter from a team or the player stating it's genuine or was signed on such-and-such a date, all the better. If it comes with a story that so-and-so was in the stands when Babe Ruth hit his 60th home run and he gave the ball to me on his deathbed saying, "It's Babe Ruth's 60th home-run ball, kid," be careful. A ball was sold with just that story for authentication recently; the ball sold for $200,000 but the buyer backed out when he heard that there was another Babe Ruth 60th-home-run ball with better authentication.

The same goes for uniforms, with the addendum that there are honest authenticators of jerseys and pants throughout the country; find one and have him authenticate your item. A friend of mine who happens to like Joe Montana and spent several years searching down the perfect Montana jersey had about ten jerseys pass through his hands; only three or four were definitely genuine, and as many were definitely counterfeit. And he took the precaution of dealing with the most reputable people he could find.

Sports art—paintings and sculpture—should only be bought if you want it in your den. It would be easier for Tom Lasorda to pass through the eye of a needle than for most sports art to double in value. And that goes for any miscellaneous memorabilia—gloves, bats, schedules, advertisements, pins, books, postcards, games, and so on—too. Buy it if you like it; don't expect it to put your son through school or a new car in the garage.

Also, if you are seriously considering sports memorabilia as an investment, find out as much as you can about the sport and its memorabilia before you invest. Learning while you buy does not work in this field.

Before You Invest

There are some facts you had better understand before seeking your fortune in cards. Most are common sense, but somehow when sports and cards are involved people start looking like the Minnesota Vikings trading enough draft picks to stock a new league for one player they don't use anyway.

The first point is a basic one. Cards are not stocks! Sure, they are a paper product and you can gain or lose money in each but that's about where the similarity ends. You wake up in the morning, check IBM in the paper and know whether you made or lost money. Moreover, for the price of a phone call you can buy more IBM or sell what you have and have a pretty good idea what the price will be for your transaction.

Cards aren't that way. Sure, you can reach for the morning price guide, but that's all that it is—a guide. It can be off by a little or a lot. Take Bo Jackson, do you seriously think that anyone in their right mind was paying catalog prices when he was released by Kansas City? Then, as we all watched him struggle to first base in spring training for the White Sox,

do you think anyone was about to pay anything like full catalog for a
Bo Jackson rookie? The truth is that you would have been lucky to
find any buyer at almost any price.

Catalogs, even the best of them, are printed long before you receive them in the mail. Prices can change by the hour so that tells you
that anyone who buys and sells cards based on prices in a magazine
or book is asking for trouble. In fact, if you base your buys only on
such price guides you are almost certain to lose money.

How can that be? It's simple: If I am willing to pay full book price
for a card you can safely assume that it's not because I like you. I'm
doing it because a card is worth more than the price guides say and I
very probably have a buyer who knows that as well. I might have
been willing to pay three, four or five times the book price for certain
cards, but if you're willing to sell those cards to me at book price that's
your loss because you didn't know the card market.

The same thing applies to selling. There are literally tons of cards
which I'd be happy to sell you for book price. I could give you dozens
(probably more like thousands) of examples in any sport. One price
guide has a 1984 Topps Mike Rozier first card at $10.00. Would I sell
that card if you offered me $3.00—you bet I would because Rozier is
going nowhere fast. The list is endless and you can begin with commons. If I had them would I gladly sell you 1969-70 O-Pee-Chee
commons? I'd do it in a second and you could have a 1971-72 Bob
Love while you're losing money and you could have it at, oh, say 75
percent of book.

How much would I pay for those cards? You want the sad truth,
well you're getting it and that's nothing. I don't want the cards any
more than I want a bunch of 1990 Fleer commons. Oh sure, you
could find a price where I'd have to take them, say 5 to 10 percent of
book, but I can assure you it won't be much because all I'm going to
do is turn around to another dealer and sell them for a few dollars
more.

It's a simple fact of life, the price guide people do not buy or sell
cards and their information is hopelessly out of date by the time you
get it. If you want to know whether a Mark Aguirre card is likely to be
more or less than a Charles Barkley of the same year then the price
guides can help. They can even give you a rough idea of how much

the cards will cost, but they are not now and never will be a guarantee that you are paying or receiving the right price.

The price guides, however, are not the most misleading information you can read before entering the market. Dealers' ads put them to shame. Look through any publication. "These are HOT," "Quantities Limited" and so on. We could spend hours on the topic of most shameless hype ever found in a card advertisement, but suffice it to say there have been some classics.

Very simply, there is no Santa Claus in the card business. If the stuff being promoted was so good, so certain to go up dramatically in price, why would anyone spend hundreds of dollars trying to convince you to buy it? The obvious answer is the correct one in that if I were that certain I wouldn't spend a dime trying to sell you the cards. I'd keep them a while, wait for the price explosion and then sell them to you.

That said, some of the offers are hard to resist as they sound so good. If you have doubts look through the publications. Is anyone offering to buy the items being promoted? After all, if they are so good other dealers would surely want a chance as well. If you're still in doubt invest a couple bucks in a few phone calls. What are dealers paying for the item you're considering? If they are not buying them that should tell you plenty about how good a purchase it would be.

Before rushing off and making your first purchase there are some additional considerations. Specifically, if you're buying for investment, how do you plan to sell your purchase at a later date after piling up your paper profits?

It's not an important consideration, it's a vital one as cards are not stocks. There is no sure market for a card and in fact there are really a number of card markets. Let's examine them as they exist at present with an eye toward their potential advantages and disadvantages.

The baseball card market for cards from 1948 to about 1980 is the active market for older cards. Widely traded, cards of this era have both a solid investor and collector following.

Prices in this market are driven more by grade and somewhat less by rarity than is the case in the historic card market. The market also experiences hot and cold spells with certain players, most significantly Mickey Mantle cards. For the more conservative investors there are still nice, solid classic cards such as the 1953 Topps Satchel Paige, which are less subject to the feeding frenzy of the moment. Good conservative buys also exist in later date (late 1960s and early 1970s) Hall of Famers who are still modestly priced.

Realistically, whatever your personality when it comes to investment, there is something for you in the period from 1948 to 1980. The key is a dealer who is an accurate grader and a fair and active buyer.

The markets for football and basketball are similar to that for baseball cards from 1948 to 1980, but smaller with less expensive prices. Instead of Mantle you can substitute Namath and Alcindor or Unitas and Erving and you have about the same situation.

It's important to understand that although football and basketball cards were made in significantly smaller quantities than baseball cards that does not mean higher prices. That's primarily due to the fact that the demand for football and basketball cards is far less than for baseball cards. It's not wise to invest with the notion that the situation will change any time soon.

A theory has also been introduced that football and basketball cards remain available in better condition than baseball cards because they were less likely to end up on that torture chamber of cards, the school playground. The theory is exactly that. Kids can damage cards whatever the weather and outside conditions. Walls can dent cards as well as playgrounds. Poor handling is possible anywhere and there is no conclusive proof that the percentage of high grade basketball and football cards is greater than that of certain baseball issues. For example, the number of truly nice 1962 Topps football cards with those easily flaked black borders is seemingly no greater than you would find among 1971 Topps baseball cards which have a similar border.

If you are going to invest in football and basketball cards, do so as a lower priced alternative to baseball cards or because you happen to like one of the other sports but not with the expectation that some day they will be priced at equal levels.

One point that can and should be made in favor of football and basketball cards is that at lower prices, the possibility of a better rate of return is real as it's always easier for a card to go from five to ten dollars than from $500 to $1000. That must, however, be balanced by the fact that the liquidity of these sports is not as great as you will find with baseball. There are still relatively few specialists in any sport other than baseball and they are more than counterbalanced by the number of dealers who do not deal actively or at all in sports other than baseball.

The hockey situation is even more specialized. The market for hockey cards is Canada and isolated dealers in the United States. Although the small supply of hockey cards is an attractive aspect of the market it can also serve to frustrate avid collecting and investing.

Another problem is condition. Serious investors tend to migrate to cards in top condition. Hockey cards from virtually any time before 1960 are notoriously difficult to find in top grade when strictly graded. Heaven knows what the young of Canada were doing with their cards, but clearly frigid Canadian winters did not keep their youngsters from extracting a heavy toll on hockey cards.

There is also a problem in getting dealers to jump into the hockey market. In part it's probably a function of lack of knowledge, but there's also a difficulty in terms of supply. No dealer can stay in business long promoting a product that he cannot buy. Hockey cards tend to be such a product. Most are still in Canada so American dealers tend to deal in current hockey cards or none at all.

The attractive thing about hockey cards is that it would not take much money or interest to see prices rise sharply much like historic baseball cards. It would cost a lot of money to buy every Mickey Mantle card known to exist, but for far less you could buy every Bobby Orr card. It's a lot of potential, but will it ever be realized?

The cards from 1980 to the current day can really be considered as a unit. Sure, the price of a baseball card might be a bit more than that of a basketball, but the name of the game is the same-rookies, rookies, rookies.

We've already said a lot about rookie cards. They have a lot of interest and potential but a couple of real problems. The first of these is that if you pick wrong you are left with quite literally nothing except a worthless piece of cardboard.

Consider this, drafting in professional sports is done by people who make their living evaluating talent. Go back and study the drafts of all respective sports over the past decade. I'll save you some time: of the four drafts, the NBA draft is probably the best indicator of a player's professional potential. The NFL draft tends to be second and the ratio of stars to busts of the first ten players selected in the NFL draft over the past decade is about 1 to 1. Even the number one player selected in the NFL draft about half the time in the last decade has become a mediocre pro or is quickly not a pro at all. In fact, statistically, the best players have been the third picks but then there are also the seventh picks who almost never work out.

If you were to analyze the hockey and, probably most tellingly, the baseball drafts you would find even worse odds. Now for a buck here and two bucks there it's no big deal. But what if you're paying $25 for the first pick in the NHL draft or what if you're paying a dollar each for 1,000 rookies of the first pick in the NFL draft? That's real money and your chances are about 50 percent that you'll lose all or most of it and even worse if you're doing your rookie buying in baseball or hockey.

If your odds of buying the right rookie are bad, your chances of selling him may be even worse. Take any card publication and look through it. Page after page, sometimes by the hundreds of chances to buy the current hot rookie cards. Compare that number to the number of full pages stating, "We Desperately Need These Hot Rookies and Will Pay Full Book To Get Them! Huge Quantities Especially Sought." Have you ever seen such an ad? Probably not, and you probably won't any time soon.

There are a number of reasons why you won't see such full pages. The main one is that the card companies produce so many cards each year that dealers rarely need any modern cards. That is not good news if you have some to sell.

The problem is even greater if you happened to buy in large quantities. You can virtually assume that the higher the price of a rookie card of recent vintage, the fewer of that card any given dealer (if you can find one who is buying at all) will want to buy. That's because the dealer knows the card is a risk, almost like the old game of pass the ticking time bomb. Your goal is not to be the person holding the bomb when it goes off and the smaller the investment the smaller the bomb. Moreover, if a dealer needs a certain rookie he can usually get it faster and at a better price from another dealer.

It's a difficult situation. Even if you can pick rookies better than the Cleveland Indians or Tampa Bay there is still that mountain of millions and millions of cards out there, plenty to fill virtually every imagi-nable demand and with millions left over in unopened cases in attics and closets all over this country. Short of a national epidemic causing cardboard to rot, the rookie card market remains the most dangerous and still, on paper at least, the most potentially rewarding and exciting of all the card markets.

Buying and Selling

Is that money burning a hole in your pocket? If it is, you're typical of someone just starting out in cards. Frequently that is when the worst mistakes are made. That's why the first word to remember is patience as, just like the old adage that some of the best trades are the ones never made, so too with some of the best card purchases.

The first problem the buyer faces is that often he has no plan whatsoever. Buyers read about the first round draft pick of the Nuggets and want him. Or they want to start with Hall of Famers from football but promptly buy the first one they see while missing a chance to obtain an older, tougher player because they ran out of money. The pitfalls are numerous.

The first thing you should do is match your budget to your goals. Let's say you have $100 a month to spend and want blue chip Hall of Famers. That's fine, but even though price guides are not reliable from a pricing standpoint you can safely assume that the $3000 King Kelly is out. Instead, check out the guides for cards that appear to fit your budget.

There's a second good reason for the

strategy as it will show you if they are really the cards you want. You might find you'd enjoy lower priced football cards even more or that your chances of completing sets would be better in basketball.

Then, there are some who have little or no idea, they just want cards and they want those cards to make money. They've heard about rookies so they seem like a good idea. We've discussed their risks elsewhere in this book. The question is can you live with something that you might well end up using as worthless packing material?

Even on a limited budget diversity has a certain nice ring to it. In fact, that's really what this book is all about as there is nothing wrong with collecting a number of sports or types of cards.

The pros and cons of some ways of assembling a collection/ investment are worth considering. Start with tradition which is the set. The complete set has long been viewed as the sure things in cards. That way you get older stars as well as promising rookies. For most it is still the logical way to go, although that thinking is changing.

One problem of the complete set is its own success. Prices on virtually all sets from the 1950s and before are out of the price range of most. That is becoming increasingly true of sets as recent as the mid-1970s. If you can't afford a complete set you have a potential problem as you can only buy them economically complete or, if you are doing it a card at a time, by purchasing the key high-priced cards first. That's not because dealers need your money, but rather because the top cards move the set in price most strongly. If a set has 10¢ commons and one $10 card which jumps to $20 your cost has increased substantially. That's how it happens too, because commons, if anything, tend to be weak links in terms of price.

Another problem in buying a card at a time is that some cards bring premiums which may or may not last long term. High numbers are such cards as they were sometimes produced in smaller quantities. They should be more expensive, but how much more is directly related to the popularity of set collecting in the future. An assortment of other cards including New York Yankees in baseball bring premiums even when they deserve "common" prices. You also have checklists, league presidents, highlights and even trophies in hockey, to mention a few cards that purchased individually are going to cost you extra money but that might be virtually thrown in as commons in a set purchased from a dealer at the right time.

All that said, and despite increasing concern about sets as investments, an older set in high grade is still a fairly secure sort of thing. It's the right idea if you don't like to have to think about your investment. Just be sure that it's correctly graded as a slight problem lowering the grade of a major card or two and your set can instantly become badly overpriced.

Another way to approach cards is with a collection of an individual player. Certainly, a Michael Jordan collection should also be a reasonably good investment. The same would apply to Gordie Howe or any major Hall of Famer. The only problem with the approach is that others might not share your enthusiasm or that you might pick a current player who might not realize his potential. Or he might have cards from the past five years or so because their production levels are so high as to make a long-term collection a more risky one financially than a collection of Ted Williams or Bart Starr.

A team collection is similar, but with a couple of twists. One is not good if you end up with the commons of the team. In basketball it might not be so bad, particularly if the team is in the Lakers class with high visibility and lots of stars. The problem comes in with one of those seemingly hopeless franchises that competes each season for a high draft pick. In such cases the collection may have a limited regional appeal, but if you have to sell out outside of the area it's likely to be at a deep discount with you facing a potentially serious loss.

Not every team is a loser. Although even the Yankees, 49ers or Celtics have down years, they are generally more than balanced out by the good. Moreover, with success comes a national following. That's good news for your collection and its value. Unfortunately, however, the more successful the team, the greater the cost, and if it takes the form of a team like the Yankees you will need a lot of money even in lower grades assuming you want to go back to the Ruth and Gehrig era.

Another method of combing a collection and an investment is the already mentioned Hall of Fame approach. In any of the sports the Hall of Famers are an interesting challenge. Trying to complete such a set gives your holdings diversity as you'll have to go back to tobacco cards to get Cobb in baseball or Jack Darragh in hockey. That gives you increased diversity and that's always a plus as all cards or even types of cards do not move uniformly in price. That way, if your

Mickey Mantles are not doing anything or perhaps even trending downward in price, their decline might be balanced by a more impressive performance by your tobacco cards.

The ultimate in Hall of Fame collecting is to go after all the Halls of Fame. Although a Hall of Fame baseball collection can be both costly and extremely hard to complete, the other sports where cards exist are still relatively inexpensive and with the exception of tobacco, hockey, and a few early football and basketball cards, not terribly hard to find on the market.

Diversification can take many forms. Perhaps you want the fun of picking your own players. Perhaps such a collection might be of players who seemed underpriced. You might feel that Willie Mays should be close to Mickey Mantle in price or that Johnny Unitas is worth a lot more than Bart Starr. Assuming the cards are of equivalent rarity you might very well be correct and you just might profit from your feelings.

If you limit yourself to Hall of Famers you could very easily just buy cards that you find appealing. That way if you think Duke Snider looks like a frog on one card you can always opt not to include Snider or perhaps pick another Snider card which is more interesting to you.

That's one of the nice things about cards. The market is really less than twenty years old as an organized affair. Just because rookies have traditionally sold at one price and second year cards of the same player at about 30 percent of the rookie card value does not mean it will stay that way forever. Moreover, just because kids once collected cards by complete sets does not mean investors and collectors have to do it the same way.

The card market's youth is also a great bonus if you happen to have more time and interest than money. Our information is not carved in anything close to granite. Each year we learn about many cards whose very existence was unknown according to the price guides. With a lot of study and hours walking aisles of card shows you can also learn that the rarity (and perhaps value) of certain cards is not correctly reflected in price guides.

Hockey stands out as a possibility on that front. Frankly, Americans have just discovered hockey cards. Our publications may be perfectly okay for cards from 1951 to the present, but they should be produced by longtime Canadian collectors and students when it comes to cards from before 1950. It's a real experience to attend a major card show with a Canadian expert on older hockey cards. They don't need catalogs, price guides or the rest. They know what a Fred Lake should be worth in comparison to a Martin Walsh and whether one type of common should bring the same price as another. Moreover, they know what prices cards should bring, and where things like Canadian tobacco cards are concerned any similarity between what they think and what an American price guide says is seemingly accidental.

The key to successful buying is knowledge. You need both knowledge of cards and market prices and knowledge regarding grading skills.

Look in any price guide and you'll see there is a big price difference between a card in Good condition and one listed as Near Mint. It's not an accident. A run down house is worth far less than one kept in top condition. So it is with anything from cars to coins. In cards the better condition item is not only more desirable, but also, with the exception of cards of recent vintage, far less common.

Let's remember, cards until about 1980 were not a lofty investment vehicle. In fact, they were a diversion for children, who treated them as you might expect. They played with them, attached them to bicycle spokes and generally engaged in a wide range of cardboard torture. Add to that the fact that cards came packaged with cigarettes, candy and gum to name a few and sat in stores all summer getting stained and you have just the beginning of a picture which is anything but pretty. Small wonder that the truly nice looking card from the 1950s is a difficult item to find, and if it happens to be from the early 1900s it's sometimes as close to a miracle as many of us will get when we hold a truly new looking Cracker Jack in our hands.

Although there is no doubt regarding the importance of grading there is a lot of misunderstanding about it. Look in price guides and you'll find general grading standards. The problem is that they do not always agree and it's not just the written words that don't agree. Take centering as evidenced by the margins on the card. Some contend a card can be Mint even if it is off center as that is the way the card was made and it's off center today not because of any wear or change but rather because of the way it was printed. Others, however, contend that a card that is poorly centered, however original, is not and cannot be Mint.

As if that isn't confusing enough, take a look at some auction catalogs or dealers' listings. You'll find not only different standards but also phrases like, "Small pin hole otherwise Ex." The phrase itself is not harmful, but the price or in the case of auctions, the suggested price tends to be a price typical of the card if it were in fact in Excellent condition. With that pin hole, however, the card is not now and never can be in Excellent condition and thus is not deserving of an Excellent price no matter how desirable.

Such things are innocent enough when compared to card restoration, trimming to sharpen corners, coloring in borders and a host of other activities designed to separate the novice from his money unfairly.

The coin market has already been through many of the same problems and expressions like "If a price is too good to be true it probably isn't" and "There is no Santa Claus in the coin (you may easily substitute "card") business" all ring true.

Moreover, at present there is no certain defense. Like the coin market, the card market has and continues to experiment with grading services. There, for a fee, a supposedly independent group examines a card and give you an opinion as to its grade. It's a decent attempt at a solution, but it is not foolproof.

If (and that's a big if) we can assume that everything about a grading service is legitimate there is still a problem. That problem is called slingshoting. The way it works is that I purchase a card I think grades "8" on a scale of 1-10. I send the card in and it comes back a grade lower than I thought. As a "7" the card is worth $100 but as an "8" it's worth $925. What I do is break it out of the holder calling it a "7" and send it back. Maybe I do it once, maybe twice, maybe many times until I get lucky and the card returns with the desired "8." It's worth the added cost to try but that leaves us with a situation where the card eventually ends up with its highest possible grade, which is not necessarily the grade most would give it and a grade which would give the card a price most would be unwilling to pay.

So if card grading services are not by definition a perfect answer, are there others? Some might suggest that finding a trustworthy

dealer would take care of things especially if that dealer agrees to buy
back cards sold to you. That's fine, but the dealer has not agreed to a
specific price. Nor has the dealer agreed to always be there. What if
the dealer dies? What if he wakes up one morning and decides to retire to become a shepherd? The list of possible reasons why the dealer
might not be there with lots of money when you need him is endless.

The answer to the grading problem is one many do not want to
hear. It's that they must learn how to grade. You cannot do it perfectly
every time, but a combination of reading the published standards in
price guides and testing yourself at shows will enable you to grade ac-
curately a reasonable percentage of the time.

To test yourself start with low priced cards. A common is a lot
better place to make a mistake than a Gordie Howe rookie simply because of price. Make a few purchases and make notes as to what
grade you thought the card was when you purchased it. Then take it
around to other dealers or experienced collectors and get their opin-
ions on the card. Do the same with purchases from your dealer to see
whether their grading stands up as well. It won't take as long as you
might think before you'll be able to understand grading standards as
they are practiced in the market. Then, grading services and dealer
buy back guarantees can be helpful, but you understand that you are
your own best defense against overgrading.

With a plan and some grading skills you are virtually ready to
start buying cards either for a collection or as an investment. There is,
however, a final thing you should do and that is get a feel for the market. You've already started by attending shows or going to local
shops. Additionally, you are probably doing some reading about
cards. That said, you can never learn enough.

A good piece of advice is to start looking at shows and advertisements in particular for cards that would be right for your collection.
Purchases aren't necessary as what you really want to do is test your
plan. Are the cards you are interested in buying readily available? If
so, they may not be that good as an investment.

You may learn of other potential problems. Perhaps your plan
was based on inaccurate prices or maybe your interests have changed
from baseball to basketball. The possibilities are numerous. The reason to test your plan is that with very few exceptions, cards are not a
good short term investment. Consequently, if you spend $100 today

on a hockey card collection only to decide in a month that you'd rather collect Hall of Fame basketball cards you'll find yourself with a good deal less than your $100 when you attempt to sell your hockey collection.

Let's assume your decision still looks good. There are many places to buy cards (mail order, auctions, shows, other collectors or investors, and so on). You need not, and probably should not, use one exclusively. The key to consider is that when buying cards it's vital that you get the important cards first. If the collection is of Willie Mays, get the rookie card first. If it's the Boston Bruins, get the Bobby Orr cards first.

There are some exceptions. Those cases are where the important cards are so tough as to be unavailable when you are starting out. In some instances, perhaps hockey Hall of Famers, we may not really know which cards are the most difficult although you could make some educated guesses. If your goal is one of each type of baseball card you might find that cards like T214s or E125s are simply not available. In fact, it might take years to find one. In that instance work on your set, but keep enough money available just in case one of the rarities does appear. While you may not know exactly how much you will need, a combination of price guides and talking to specialists will usually give you some idea as to what even the most elusive of cards would be expected to bring at auction. That's why learning about cards is so important. There is no book out there to tell you exactly what cards are going to be the most difficult to find. But there are specialists and there is your own experience which is why you should attend all the shows and read all the publications you can including the advertisements.

Why read advertisements? The reason is simple. They are an excellent way to see what is on the market. In a given week a state like California might have twenty shows. You can't attend them all even though it might be fun. With advertisements you can get an idea what dealers around the nation and around the world are both buying and selling. That's vital information as if dealers are trying to buy it, the card is probably a good investment. If they aren't selling it, it's probably rare and should be a high priority card to buy. Over years, you can well become an expert in your own field and that's your goal, in addition to attaining a great collection.

SELLING

Let's face it. Unless you plan to be buried with them, some day you or a loved one are going to sell your cards. More appropriately, you are going to attempt to sell them. Most think the process is easy. Nothing could be further from the truth. More often than not, your first attempt will show that your treasures are someone else's trash or at least that's how they act.

With auctions, dealers, and other collectors, you'd think this selling thing would be easy. Brace yourself, it can well be the most discouraging part of a baseball card investment and sometimes it seems like it's not your fault.

Take one case. A Gordie Howe rookie in Excellent condition and purchased for well under "book" price. The card was consigned to one of the most well known auctions in America with a minimum bid price of its alleged book value. It not only didn't sell, there was not even a nibble. Then the card crossed the country going to a number of large shows. Again no reaction. It was not a grading problem as no one argued with the grade or even that it was priced right for the grade. Finally, on a lark the card was consigned to a lesser auction where it sold for 30 percent over the so-called "book" price. If there is a moral in the story it's probably that you never really know for sure what it will take to produce your price on a card.

A second lot involved some 10,000 cards of a rookie who became an all-star. Bought right (specifically at 10¢ a card) it should have resulted in a fortune. Instead, the cards are still unsold. The fact is that the lot was too large for the market. The player, while a star, never really got hot in terms of demand and the owner was unwilling to break up the lot. Even so, he did everything right and was lucky that the player became a star. The collector should have made money. Perhaps if the player continues to be an all-star the owner will, but it's been five years and could easily be another five.

Take the two stories together and a picture is emerging. The picture is not that pretty, but you had better recognize it. Cards are not very liquid as investments. They are hard to sell, especially if you want top dollar and you want it now.

That is lesson one, assume it will take some time if you expect anything close to top dollar. A forced sale that has to be done quickly is likely to produce a serious financial loss unless you've had the cards for an extended period of time and unless they've gone up dramatically in price. Even then, you're probably going to sell them too cheaply.

To seriously assess your cards for sale the first point is that you have to be realistic. Are your cards featured in advertisements of those cards dealers want to buy like a Cracker Jack Joe Jackson? If so, then your life is easy. You can happily put them in an auction or take dealer offers accepting the best one.

If, however, your cards are not appearing as a regular on those lists of wanted to buy you may have a problem. Get some offers. Forget the book price as a dealer cannot buy at book price and then sell for the same price. If he has a customer for the cards you might get offered 80 percent of the book or likely sale price. If not, the offers are going to be much less.

What you'll receive may well be a function of how desireable your cards are. If there are some great items like Mantle rookies and Ruth Goudeys then they can be used as leverage to get a major auction to take all of your holdings. That's why the key card in any collection is so vitally important. Without a card or cards that everyone wants, your situation is closer to that of the person with 10,000 rookies of a star no one wants.

All things being equal, an auction tends to be the best way to get top prices for the average person. As a creative second, striking a deal with a trustworthy dealer to handle them on consignment is another option. Taking out your own advertisements in hobby papers ranks third along with getting your own table at a show and selling them yourself.

Do you notice something missing from that list? You should, it's direct sale to dealers. Why is that missing? The simple reason is that matter of liquidity. Far too many dealers in all card markets today cannot handle a big sale financially and virtually no one wants to buy cards of recent years. If your collection warrants it, you can find a dealer who is interested, but if you think you can pass your mistakes along to a dealer at a profit forget it—you might as well expect to make a killing in Las Vegas by betting on the Indians.

Probably your best chance with dealers is if you have a specialized collection and know the important dealers in the area of specialization. Beyond that, Hall of Famers and high grades are the next most likely elements to get your cards top dollar from dealers and that is assuming you have older cards. If what you've got is box after box of modern rookies and commons then unless you've got a friend you've got a problem.

There are some who would have you believe that cards are simple. They would have you think that you merely plop down your money and await riches. People have made money in cards. They bought right, they knew how to sell their cards, they had great dealers and they probably worked very hard to make themselves expert in all aspects of cards. There is no other way. It's not the stock market, it's not real estate, it takes work and unless you're willing to put in that work, your only hope is dumb luck and it's dumb to hope for that.

Contrary Investing

If you think beyond the sports-card market to the greater memorabilia market for a moment, you might just conclude that you've been going at this card-investing thing all wrong. The things that are valuable today are not the things that people kept because they were concerned about their future value; the things that are valuable today are the things people *used*, with little or no regard for future value. Fiestaware. Depression glass. Barbie dolls and Buck Rogers rayguns. Rayon Hawaiian shirts. Refrigerator magnets. '57 Chevies. Fender Stratocaster guitars. Earl Torgeson autograph-model gloves. Waring blenders. None of these things were hoarded at the time by collectors or investors because they were too common, too run-of-the-mill. Instead, they became part of the everyday fabric of our lives, while the collectors collected and the investors invested in . . .

Coins and stamps. Rolls of silver dollars and sheets of safety-patrol commemoratives. People lined up at the post office for sheets and plate blocks and put away rolls of uncirculated dollars, certain—100 percent SURE—that they were just the ticket to put Junior and Juniette through college.

So college time rolled around, and those sheets of safety-patrol commemoratives were good for sticking on the application-form envelope and that was about it, and the silver dollars were good for weighting down the tarpaulin so the wind wouldn't get underneath it and that was about it, because EVERYONE had bought sheets of safety-patrol stamps and rolls of uncirculated dollars for the appreciation potential, and no one bothered to wonder whether anyone would actually want to pay big money for these things twenty-five years hence.

The things that people collect for value are rarely the things that people subsequently want. Collector/investors would have been better off going down to the local Gambles/Skogmo store come Christmas-shopping time and buying two of every present—one to give and one to put away. But no one did, and the results are obvious.

Which brings us to modern-day sports cards. The number of people buying these things to stick away on a closet shelf as a hedge against inflation and a sure-fire college fund is enormous. There are perhaps 16 million card collectors, and you can bet that 15.9 million of them have these long white boxes sitting on the shelf in the hall closet, aging, like wine of some uncertain vintage, and the people who own the long white boxes take occasional wistful stares at them and wonder: When are they going to explode in value? When are people going to start clamoring for these very sets? When are they going to make me rich?

Never, probably. Everyone who wants one has one, and there are enough of them being kept in hermetically sealed, nearly perfect shape to ensure that they'll never be worth $52,000 the way the 1952 Topps set is. Sure, there are investment strategies you can pursue that will guide you away from these tar pits, but the bulk of sports cards being issued today are not going to be worth significantly more fifteen years from now.

Scary? Not really. But it ought to make you think: Why buy what everyone else is buying? Why buy collectibles? Calling something contemporary a collectible virtually ensures that it won't be collectible in another couple of years. Instead, consider collecting the stuff that has proven to be collectible, and valuable, over time. Collect —and invest in—the dross, the crapola, the stuff of everyday life.

It makes sense, certainly as much sense as buying a case of Pacific Football Flashcards and figuring it'll someday trade out to a semester at Cornell. It's contrary, of course, but the contrary path has proven to be the way to go in the collectibles-investing field.

But there's so much dross, especially in sports cards, and some of the dross is so much drossier than others. Where do you start? Here are a few contrary-investing suggestions.

STICKERS

Starting in 1981, four companies—Topps, O-Pee-Chee, Fleer and Panini—made sets of baseball stickers. They were sold in small packets or packages with gum, usually four for 15 cents or six for a quarter. Albums to house them were sold separately. And, as you might expect, they were low-rent, nasty little things, and kids stuck them into their albums with alacrity.

How perfect! How utterly, disgustingly perfect! Here you have a sports product that was designed to be used, and as soon as it was used, its value was destroyed. No one wants a sticker that's already been stuck. The only real value is in unstuck stickers and unstickered albums. And let me tell you: Both are hard to find, and disgustingly cheap.

I particularly like the Fleer Star Stickers, which were issued from 1981-88. A lot of them look like cards, and very nice cards; they even have card backs that you could crack and peel. Other years they looked like other stickers—which is to say, trashy—but even then they have a certain greasy attractiveness. I also like Topps Stickercards, which were the company's last fling at sticker success. These have an adhesive-backed photo on one side and a interesting little card on the other. There are all kinds of combinations of stickers and cards, which makes collecting a complete set with all varieties essentially impossible. The best you can do is a full run of stickers and a full run of cards. There were football Stickercards, too, which reminds me: Buy football and hockey stickers. They were made in even fewer quantities than baseball stickers, and are even harder to find.

TOPPS BIG CARDS

Topps is renowned for just flinging something out on the market with little concern for what you'd think were basic marketing facts —like whether the market actually wants it, for instance. Topps Big cards were one of those issues that got flung and stuck around for a while, and wound up being a really interesting run of cards.

Bigs were designed to be a modern-date update of the 1955-56 Topps style: horizontal format, two photos, cartoon backs. And they worked; all three years they riffed off of the '55-56 theme with style and charm.

Bigs were also issued in series—three series a year, one for each month of the summer. It looked like the perfect marketing strategy: a series a month of neat-looking cards for each month the kids are out of school. And Topps Bigs started out like gangbusters, like a real Topps smash success, like the bubble gum shaped like a human thumb, only better. People were clamoring for the stuff, paying big bucks for it; they just couldn't get enough of Topps Big Baseball.

But that lasted about as long as it took for the cards to get everywhere, and Topps found out soon enough why it got out of the issuing-cards-in-series business to start with: The last series invariably got lost. Third-series Bigs never made it onto shelves in any quantity, unless they were warehouse shelves. By 1990, second-series cards weren't even making it out to retail, and it was then that Topps pulled the plug on the whole endeavor.

There are some very scarce issues in this run of sets. Anything from 1990, especially second and third series, is worth picking up. Third-series 1989 is very tough, and even 1988 third-series cards are hard to find. Prices (currently in the $15-$20 range per set) don't reflect the scarcity.

Believe it or not, Topps Bigs were precedent-setting cards. Their style predated Topps Kids cards and even something as snooty as Fleer Ultra. Their three-series format was later copied by Topps Stadium Club. They're attractive, fun cards, and you can't help but like them.

MCDONALD'S FOOTBALL CARDS

Football cards were in a funk in 1986. Topps was the only company issuing football cards, and it wasn't doing a good job at all of issuing an interesting, collectible set. Football-card collectors were about as common as black truffles, and about as active. That's why what football-card collectors there were got so excited when they heard McDonald's would be issuing a nationwide series of regional football-card sets.

The sets were issued so that any place that had an NFL team in its vicinity got a set of those players. Places that were a long ways from any NFL team got an all-star set.

The cards are oversized and were given away with food purchases. On the bottom of each card is a coupon that had to be scratched off and then redeemed for a different food premium or other prize each week. As the premiums changed from week to week, so did the color of the scratch-off tab. There were four color tabs—black, orange, blue and green—and therefore four sets for each team.

Collectors loved these cards because they posed a real challenge, and a myriad of ways to collect. The complete master set consists of each color-tabbed set for each team, plus the four all-star sets, and is virtually impossible to assemble. Collectors have also tried to assemble one set from each team regardless of color tab, and complete color-tab runs of individual teams. There are some fantastic scarcities among the color-tab sets, and some other tab sets that are common as dirt. Complicating everything are the tabs. If they're taken off, scratched off or defaced the grade of the cards drops to Fair at best.

As time passes and football-card collectors become more sophisticated about their roots, the McDonald's sets will take on more and more prominence. Prices for the cards have remained stagnant since an initial flurry of popularity, so now is as good a time as any to buy. There are usually sets for sale in the classified ads of *Sports Collectors Digest*. The important things to remember are the tab-color scarcities (any good price-guide book will list them) and tab condition.

MOTHER'S COOKIES CARDS

Since 1984 some of the nicest, most attractive cards around haven't been issued by a cardmaker but by Oakland-based Mother's Cookies.

Mother's makes team sets for most of the teams in the West

and Southwest, and individual player sets it sneaks one card at a time into bags of its cookies. The first 25,000 or so people through the gates on Mother's Cookies Card Day get 20 of the 26 cards in the set and a certificate to send in for six more cards—not necessarily the cards they need to complete their set. The idea behind this is to encourage trading, but what it really does is keep a lot of sets incomplete.

Mother's is better than most companies at keeping control of its sets and minimizing the amount that sneaks out the back door of the printing plant. That 25,000-set limit is just about an absolute limit. When you consider that, and further consider that all these companies that talk such big talk about limited-editions with their products are actually talking about 150,000 at the least, Mother's Cookies cards sound great. And they show some of the best players in the game: Jose Canseco, Mark McGwire, Darryl Strawberry, Eric Davis, Nolan Ryan, Ruben Sierra, Ken Griffey, Jr.

Just for scarcity's sake stick to Mother's Cookies team sets, though the individual-player sets are nice if you can get them cheaply. Even older sets of these cards aren't really moving now, so you should be able to get some nice, scarce, early cards of Canseco and Griffey for less than $20. And that's what this contrary-investing thing is all about.

COSTACOS BROTHERS POSTERS

When you think of contrary investing focusing on things that are designed to be used and used up and then discarded, another perfect item for contrary investors is sports posters. Posters are aimed squarely at the prime use-it-up-and-toss-it market: kids ages 7 to 18. They buy posters, stick them on their walls, and when they get tired of that player or that poster or the tape lets loose they take it down and toss it and put a new one up.

Again, how perfect! Right now, only people who collect all the items of a certain superstar are buying posters and keeping them in collectible condition, and there aren't many of those collectors and they're only focusing on their one player.

The best posters are made in Seattle by a company called Costacos Brothers. The posters are graphically fun; for instance, one recent poster, entitled "Kevin Mitchell—Master Blaster," shows the Seattle slugger surrounded by bats painted up to look like dynamite. There have been Costacos Brothers posters that show Karl Malone jamming a basketball into a mailbox, Kirby Puckett posing in a wrecking yard, Eric Dickerson dressed up like RoboCop, Eric Davis dressed like Sam Spade, Dominique Wilkins flying through The Hilight Zone, and more. The company's posters are neat, and because they're neat, they've been stuck up everywhere. And because they've been stuck up everywhere, they're instantly collectible, and nobody knows it.

These posters are even easy to buy. Your local discount store or card shop ought to have them, for about $5 each. You don't need to buy twenty of each player, or even five or ten of each. Just stick away a couple every now and then and be prepared to wait. You may have to wait a while, but people will eventually come around to the notion of these posters as collectibles. Which they are.

KENNER STARTING LINEUP STATUES

The beauty of these has been tarnished somewhat by the fact that Kenner sells complete sets directly to collectors, but these blister packs combining a bendable, posable football, basketball or baseball player statue and a card are still great candidates for contrary-investment status. The statues are like GI Joe action figures or Teenage Mutant Ninja Turtles; they're meant to be played with, and even if more than you'd like have been set aside and put away a whole bunch have been turned into sandbox toys, which is exactly what you want to see.

Like most truly mass-market items, with Starting Lineups the commons are the stars, since every kid wants a Starting Lineup of Michael Jordan or Ken Griffey, Jr., and not everyone has the hots for Glenn Braggs or Muggsy Rogues. This makes picking the right ones to buy something of a crapshoot. You want statues that no one wants right now but that someone will care about fifteen or twenty years hence. If you have trouble figuring out what that translates to in the here and now, when you're trying to make intelligent buying decisions on this stuff, just scope out your local toy store and scarf up whatever Starting Lineups they put on clearance—and believe me, they will put these things on clearance. You're buying dross, remember, so you have to look for dross.

SPORTFLICS

In 1986, the baseball-card world, that small, pathetic thing, was rocked by the announcement of a new product: Sportflics. The cards would have full-color backs with player biographies, photos and statistics, and the fronts would have three-count-'em-three photographs arranged through a process called lenticular technology that changed the photograph when the card was tilted. Sportflics dubbed the technology "Magic Motion," and the first significant gimmick cards of the baseball-card era were born.

Sportflics were ahead of their time. They were arguably the first high-end cards. Since they were expensive cards to produce, packs and sets cost more than average baseball cards. They weren't made in the quantities of regular baseball cards, either, simply because the cards were expensive to make and the product wasn't a true mass-market item. Their color backs, high-style design and intelligently written biographies set the standard for the other cardmakers to follow. And they were box-office bombs.

Why? People saw them as gimmick cards. Collectors have been able to transcend that notion with Action Packed and Collector's Edge football cards—no less gimmick cards than Sportflics—but at the early stage of collector sophistication when Sportflics were released, there was no getting over that perception.

The cards also lacked most big-name rookies, though there is a great card that pictures six rookies, among them Jose Canseco and Mike Greenwell. At that time the market was so rookie-oriented that anything that didn't have enough of the right kind of rookie was immediately black-balled. And that's what happened to Sportflics.

Sportflics sets are relatively expensive for dross: $35 to $40. But that's their issue price; they haven't really budged in the intervening years, though there has been some recent price movement on the inaugural set.

Like Topps Big cards, Sportflics will someday be recognized as an innovative, fun line of cards, and people will pay significantly more money for them than they are paying now. That's an alluring bottom line.

NBA HOOPS SHEETS

One of the No. 1 things to look for when choosing contrary investments is relative scarcity versus absolute scarcity. For instance, if you were told that NBA Hoops made 25,000 Chicago Bulls card sheets, you'd think, "25,000? Why, that isn't scarce at all." But when you figure that NBA Hoops may have printed 7 million NBA Hoops cards of Chicago Bulls, that makes the Hoops sheets relatively scarce, and very desirable.

The sheets of cards have been given away by NBA Hoops in the various NBA arenas for the last two basketball seasons. They're perforated sheets consisting of the NBA Hoops cards of that team's players, perhaps a special card or two, and a card showing the sponsor of the giveaway night. The special cards, cards that didn't appear in the regular set, make the sheets necessities for completists, and the fact that there are so many ways for the sheets to not make it into collectors' hands in collectible condition—they could be thrown away at the arena or dinged up on the way from the arena home or separated into individual cards—make them something worth seeking out in collectible condition.

Some of the sheets were also made available to the public through mail-in offers, diminishing their worth somewhat (Bulls sheets in particular), but otherwise the sheets are a nice mix of relative scarcity, desirability, and value ($5 to $10 per sheet, with only a few exceptions). And these comments apply to Upper Deck's in-stadium commemorative sheets saluting the Heroes of Baseball as well.

But while the subject is NBA Hoops, there are two more NBA Hoops products that have the makings of excellent contrary investments. In 1990–91, Hoops produced a neat line of 8×10 photos called NBA Hoops Action Photos. The photos were designed to be sent to players and autographed, and they were perfect for that. Unfortunately, they weren't perfect for much of anything else. They were too big to be stored and collected like cards, and they were too small to be hung like posters. As a result, they weren't big sellers and were discontinued after that one year.

The photos were sold in national all-star packs and regional team packs, with the national all-star packs being much more popular; as a result, the tough photos are like the toughest Kenner Starting Lineup statues: players that otherwise would be commons. Michael Jordans and Patrick Ewings are the easiest photos to track down, and Paul Pressey and Wayman Tisdale are the hardest to find.

NBA Hoops Action photos were primarily a retail product; therefore, it's hard to find dealers who carry even the relatively common national photo packs. When they do, though, the prices are cheap: Only a couple of bucks for the national all-star packs, and less for the regional packs.

One word of caution: Picture packs have never been big-money items. Even the scarce Jay Publishing picture packs of the '50s and '60s have not taken off in value, nor do they appear likely to. But the NBA Hoops Action Photos—and to a lesser extent, their baseball cousins, the T&M Sports 8×10s—are certainly capable of changing that.

The other products of NBA Hoops' parent company, Impel Marketing/SkyBox International, that have some potential are its basketball and baseball Collect-A-Books. Collect-A-Books, the brainchild of *Ball Four* Author Jim Bouton, are card-size, kid-oriented player biographies that span several pages and include cartoons and statistics. They were sold several Collect-A-Books to a small box and several boxes to a series, so it was not hard to complete a set. They were bought and broken up by dealers, spurned by collectors and bought up by kids, but not in such grant quantities that Impel felt compelled to continue the product after 1991.

Since they have not been collected at all Collect-A-Books are perfect for the contrary investor. You can find complete sets for a couple of dollars, and should be able to complete the entire run for less than $10. They're not going to make you rich in and of themselves, but they're also not going to make you poor buying them.

DONRUSS POP-UPS

If the standard for judging some of these contrary products is that if they're used the way they're intended they become worthless, Donruss Pop-Ups certainly fill the bill. They were made by

Donruss from 1987-90 and sold in packs with what used to be Donruss' oversized Action All-Stars, downsized and called merely Donruss All-Stars.

Pop-Ups were die-cut player cards with punch-out, stand-up stadium backgrounds. They were sold in packs that were absolute rummage sales. In addition to the long, narrow Pop-Ups and the card-sized All-Stars, Pop-Up packs included that long-time Donruss staple, the puzzle piece (a truly contrary contrary investment), and all for about 35 cents. Kids would buy the packs, toss the puzzle piece, keep the All-Star cards, and punch out the Pop-Ups. There were no real Pop-Up collectors. As a result, there's a shortage of pristine Mint Pop-Ups—and another opportunity for the contrary investor.

Like all the other contrary investments that have been discussed in this chapter, Pop-Ups are hard to find and cheap. If you can find unopened boxes of the stuff and put them away, so much the better. This is one issue where there's likely be a premium for unopened product in the years to come.

There's no telling on how long it may take for people to start clamoring for Pop-Ups; ten to fifteen years is a safe guess. If you can buy the stuff cheaply enough and afford to sit on it that long, you'll be rewarded.

OTHER-SPORT CARDS

These will be dealt with at a later date. Basically, they should be viewed as contrary from the get-go, but not necessarily valuable because of it.

MISCELLANEOUS JUNK

Returning to the more established realms of baseball, football, basketball and hockey cards once again, there have been a lot of companies that have come up with the greatest sports-collectible marketing idea since bubble gum, raised the capital, turned the idea into reality, and found that no one wants to buy into their idea and nobody cares. This is pretty traumatic for these companies, and they usually fold up quietly after providing us with one or two years of their product, which often isn't all that horrible but certainly isn't up there with bubble gum as far as innovation is concerned. Just look at what the last couple of years have wrought: MVP player pins with baseball and football cards. Flipp Tips hand-held player flip books. Tri-Cards laser-etched plastic-laminated cards. Homers collectible baseball cookies with cards. Starshots stand-up baseball buttons. Magnetables magnet-backed player photos. Baseball Wit card games. Chicagoland Processing silver rounds. Some of this stuff is going to turn out to be valuable and collectible. Some is destined for yard sales and Salvation Army stores. Some of it is going to continue to be dross forever and ever.

As for the items I just mentioned, the Homers cookies are pretty lame; they weren't very good cookies and the cards inside were too easy to buy on the secondary market. The Flipp Tips are bizarre and were clearance-racked not too long ago, which is always a good sign. The company that makes Tri-Cards isn't dead yet, but it's close. The guy who founded the company thought up the idea for Starshots, which is another good sign. Starshots and the MVP pins are a little esoteric, but they have crossover appeal to pin collectors as well as baseball-card collectors, so they might be worth picking up—in their original blister packs, if you please—if you can find them. The silver rounds are the rolls-of-silver-dollars thing all over again. The Baseball Wit games absolutely vanished from the face of the earth; buy them if you can find them. Same with the Magnetables, which have crossover appeal to the growing legions of people who collect—and I am not making this up—refrigerator magnets.

These are merely examples, and just the tip of the iceberg as far as sports-card dross is concerned. Keep an eye out for this stuff as it's released. Scan the lists of new issues published in the hobby periodicals. If you find items that are not meant to be collectibles right out of the chute, are meant to be used and used up, are designed to work their way into the fabric of everyday life, and are sort of lame on top of everything else, you may have found a winner. Remember, the whole idea of contrary investing is finding out what no one wants now but everyone is going to want later. You have to rotate your thinking 180 degrees to be successful at it. If you can pull that off, you'll find some real success in this game.

Your Best Investment

Money, money, money. It's a shame when you see long lines at shows waiting for free items to sell. It's a shame we've spent most of the time in this book talking about how to make money and not how to have fun.

Often times people mention the market in the same breath as other hobbies. Frequently they discuss coins and how that market turned into a profit driven one after having been the hobby of the young for years.

I remember it well. As a youngster we had Mantle and Mays, but we avidly sought things like 1909-S pennies and 1932-D quarters. Yes, if we found those or other coins we might make money, but more often they would have been used to fill a hole in our books where we kept our coins.

In the 1980s the rare coin market turned into a market driven solely (or so it seemed) by profit. Dealers stopped talking to the little buyer, started wearing three-piece suits and started talking to their investors. It wasn't a pretty sight for a host of reasons.

Armed with graphs and stories, all they seemed to know was whether Morgan dollars were up 40 percent in the previous six months or not. The story behind the Morgan dollar or other coins got lost in the shuffle. Seminars dealt with investing and not with history or art found on coins or paper money. It was really a great loss, and along the way the fun that had been a large part of a good hobby seemed to disappear.

We haven't reached the stage yet where fun is the missing part of the hobby, but we may be getting there. After all, it's hard to laugh when you're losing money you viewed as savings. The pain is lessened greatly when it happens to be money you were going to spend on a round of golf or a fishing trip.

It's ironic as there are people out there who insist on spending money without ever learning what it is they are buying.

The signs are all around. Price guides are read more religiously than anyone ever imagined. Grading services seem to pop up with some regularity. The TV and national press run advertisements sometimes with famous athletes talking about the staggering increases in value in rookies. Long lines form for promo cards at the national while virtually every pack in every store is a mini-lottery with the possibility of a valuable and rare autograph (as if the normal cards weren't enough).

Taken separately all these events seem harmless enough, but all are new, all are products of the great card boom and there is no corresponding increase in information about cards.

Go to any book store. I did and found eight price guides of various types on cards. I found a grand total of two books worth mentioning on baseball cards, one on football and none on hockey and basketball. If I had limited it to cards from before 1948 (about which we know the least) there were probably less than 20 pages as opposed to roughly 4000 pages of prices.

Consider it this way. The buyer is increasingly becoming a spectator in the card market. Someone is only too happy to tell you what to buy, how much to pay, what grade the card is and if you really like to lose money they will even buy it for you!

The old phrase, "If you want something done right do it yourself" comes readily to mind in this flood of offers. There is simply no substitute for knowledge when it comes to consumer protection. Nor is there anything like that knowledge to enable you to appreciate the cards you have and the cards you want to obtain.

There was a phrase in coins that suggested that a good collection was the best investment. Too bad somewhere along the line that hobby forgot the little kid who wanted a 30¢ Buffalo nickel in favor of the doctor who wanted to invest $50,000 and didn't have the time to do it himself. The result of that neglect is that the coin market today is to put it gently, in the tank. Oh sure, it may come back, but the record investor-inspired prices are now down 50 percent or so and a lot of dealers are looking for new lines of work with their investors/clients out of luck.

There's a message in what happened to coins and that market. The collector, the specialist, the buyer, with those well worn pages in their books about coins, suffered little if at all. In fact, many are happy now that prices are down as they can buy more coins.

Some might think it can't happen in cards. In fact, it has been happening for the last couple of years but there is very little market coverage, what with the flood of new issues. In *Making Money with Baseball Cards* (Bonus Books), price trends were shown and they did not always go up. A similar charting of cards in recent years would almost certainly show the same thing.

For years, the controlling forces in the coin market felt it was bad for business to suggest that prices could go down. Even to the present day their coverage of market declines is weak at best. One major price decline was generally considered merely a tightening of grading standards meaning your old $100 item in top grade was now a $50 item in nearly top grade. For those who call dealers wanting cards only in "Mint" condition there is a serious lesson there.

Ten, maybe even five years ago investing in cards was a sure thing. As long as adults could be convinced it wasn't totally absurd to spend money on the toys of their youth cards had a future just like toys, dolls and similar items. For one generation it was Lou Gehrig, for another Gordie Howe and for still another Julius Erving. All brought that flood of feeling from a happier, less pressured time. You can sell that to adults even if the names are Al Dewsbury and Jimmy Wynn. At a time when people were just happy to get rid of the cards cluttering attics and children's rooms you couldn't lose.

Today it's different. You can spend big money and get burned. You get forests of hype about issues no one understands or wants. For your own protection you need to know something about cards and the card market.

But there's more. When we discuss learning we're not talking about physics or a foreign language. We're discussing the history of sports and the history of cards that depict the people who best played those sports. It's something well short of heavy reading.

We've geared this book to those wanting profits and not necessarily pleasure from their cards. That's because it's already been shown that that will generate greater interest thus confirming some of our worst fears. But you can dare to be different.

Sure, cards can be profit vehicles, but they can also be entertaining, educational and an almost pure reflection on the country and its people and that's fun.

Let's check a few examples. If you doubt the influence of television take a long look at 1955 Bowman baseball cards. Okay, so they are not exactly attractive. But they are accurate as 1955 televisions were not exactly sleek space age models either. Then look at 1966-67 Topps hockey cards and guess what—the blooming television is back.

Now take an early Bowman card, the sometimes slightly stiff color portrait type, and compare that to virtually any card issued around 1971. It sure wouldn't take a genius to figure out which card reflects the culture of the late 1960s and those are just a couple of examples.

Remember, just because cards were issued in sets is no reason why you have to collect or invest in them by set. For investment reasons we have already suggested that you ignore the set concept. That sort of disorder may bother some, but it really is so much better than simply buying one card after another by number. Great art isn't made by painting by numbers so why should great collections be made that way?

There is really a lifetime of interetsing cards out there waiting to be discovered. Problem is they aren't all good or even fair investments, but then neither are a lot of other things which happen to be fun.

We've already talked about styles of cards, but there are more possibilities. Cards aren't equal by any stretch of the imagination. Some are pretty, some are pretty ugly and some are pretty funny and if you don't worry about investment, you can collect some of every type.

Back before Fleer got serious about its spot in the hearts of Wall Street investors they issued some hysterical cards. It should have become a tradition. Mickey Hatcher with an oversized glove, Jay Johnstone and his Budweiser umbrella. It was funny stuff on baseball cards and it still makes for good time collecting.

And then there were the uglies. Actually there still are uglies, but executives from the companies have a way of getting offended when you tell them their cards are ugly as sin.

Ugly isn't limited to baseball. Take the early Parkhurst hockey sets. Too bad they have so many important rookies in them because otherwise we could ignore them totally. As it is we're stuck shelling out $1000 or $2000 for rookies of Gordie Howe, Rocket Richard and others despite the fact that they are absolutely god-awful-looking little things. Really, like stick figures in hockey attire and these things are now worth thousands of dollars, but you could get an ugly common for a lot less.

Of the major sports football has always had a special place when it comes to the unusual. In fact, you could easily put together a collection of hysterical football cards involving everything from hair styles to poses, especially quarterbacks suspended in mid air for no apparent reason, and many others.

In the early 1960s the Philadelphia Gum Company made a number of important football cards as Topps was in or out of the football market depending on the league and other mysterious forces that influence Topps. The 1964 Philadelphia Gum Company set is a relatively harmless initial effort of 198 cards. The problem came from the Cleveland Browns. Take a look at any of the Browns. There in all their glory are Jimmy Brown, Galen Fiss, Gary Collins and the others depicted in what would appear to be a parking lot. Whether standing in front of parked cars is better than absurd poses is a matter for the ages, but it sure is unusual yet somehow typical of about a decade of football funnies committed to cardboard.

That does not by definition mean that the 1964 Philadelphia Gum Company set will be a good investment. In fact, for football cards it will probably be about average. What it does mean is that it's a set that is interesting and for those who like old cars and football players in parking lots a fun set.

The point of these examples (and there are many others) is that learning about cards not only improves your chances in terms of investment, but also enhances your possibilities for enjoyment.

That's why knowledge in the end is your best investment in cards. If you want to make money it will help you do that whether you are trying to pick rookies or buy previously unknown sleepers at bargain basement prices. If, however, satisfaction and enjoyment of a great hobby are equally interesting to you a solid background in cards will enable you to pick those cards which best satisfy your interests and needs. Either way, it's information that paves the road to success in cards.

Buy/Sell Recommendations For Baseball Cards From 1948-1979

In this chapter we will examine all the Topps and Bowman baseball cards produced from 1948-1979. I will give you my specific recommendations on what cards you should be adding to your portfolio.

As far as selling I wouldn't hold any cards from 1948-1979 that are below near mint condition. Cards from 1980 to date should only be acquired in mint condition, the only exception might be a few very expensive modern cards in nm/mt condition.

All recommendations are made with a holding period of three to five years in mind. Some of the recommended cards may show very nice appreciation in a shorter time frame, but that's a little bonus. MOST COLLECTIBLES ARE NOT SHORT-TERM INVESTMENTS. If they are, you're usually dealing with very speculative issues. We are not here to speculate, but to show you how to make money with your investment dollars. Anyone who tells you that you can get rich quick is usually trying to separate you from your hard-earned money. If it's that easy, why don't *they* keep the cards and make all the money themselves. Usually it's because their recommendations are not that good.

For those of you who can hold five to ten years, the profits can sometimes become very impressive to say the least.

1948 BOWMAN

The first Bowman set is not as popular as one would expect for a first issue. The cards are small and black-and-white, which may hurt the value somewhat. Cards from this year are scarce in top grades. I recommend the purchase of cards from this year in near mint or better condition only.

BEST BETS:
#3 Ralph Kiner
#4 Johnny Mize
#5 Bob Feller
#6 Yogi Berra
#8 Phil Rizzuto
#17 Enos Slaughter
#18 Warren Spahn
#36 Stan Musial
#38 Red Schoendienst
#45 Hank Sauer
#47 Bobby Thomson

Buy the following in mint condition only:
#1 Bob Elliott
#48 Dave Koslo

Commons from this year would be a good buy in nm/mt condition or better, mainly because commons as they are called are not common, but actually pretty scarce in top grades.

Sell all cards in less than strict near mint condition.

1949 BOWMAN

Bowman's second card set was greatly expanded from 1948. It contains quite a few key cards, some variations and a high number series. Buy the following cards in near mint or better condition only.

BEST BUYS:
#23 Bobby Doerr
#24 Stan Musial
#26 George Kell
#27 Bob Feller
#29 Ralph Kiner
#33 Warren Spahn
#50 Jackie Robinson
#60 Yogi Berra
#65 Enos Slaughter
#84 Roy Campanella
#85 Johnny Mize
#98 Phil Rizzuto
#100 Gil Hodges
#110 Early Wynn
#214 Richie Ashburn
#224 Satchel Paige
#226 Duke Snider
#233 Larry Doby
#238 Bob Lemon

Buy the following in mint condition only:
#1 Vern Bickford
#240 Norm Young

There are also some good buys in some of the cheaper star cards, such as #18 Bobby Thomson, #35 Vic Raschi, #47 Johnny Sain, #67 Alvin Dark, and #70 Carl Furillo just to name a few. Cheaper cards tend to do better percentagewise when they take off. But, of course, the key cards are always in the most demand, which is something you always have to keep in mind when you're ready to sell.

Sell all cards in less than strict near mint condition.

1950 BOWMAN

This was the last year of this size card and was one of the first issues to have low number cards that were very difficult to locate. A nice colorful set that is definitely difficult to locate in high grades.

BEST BETS:
#6 Bob Feller
#8 George Kell
#19 Warren Spahn
#21 Pee Wee Reese
#22 Jackie Robinson
#23 Don Newcombe
#32 Robin Roberts
#33 Ralph Kiner
#35 Enos Slaughter
#40 Bob Lemon
#43 Bobby Doerr
#46 Yogi Berra
#62 Ted Kluszewski
#71 Red Schoendienst
#75 Roy Campanella
#77 Duke Snider
#84 Richie Ashburn
#98 Ted Williams
#112 Gil Hodges
#139 Johnny Mize
#148 Early Wynn
#220 Leo Durocher
#232 Al Rosen

Buy the following in mint condition only:
#1 Mel Parnell
#252 Billy Demars

Also buy low number commons #1-#72 in nm/mt condition or better. For you bargain hunters or someone on a smaller budget, again look at the cheaper star cards like #3 DiMaggio, #79

When you consider that Ken Griffey, Jr., could be the best all-around centerfielder to happen along since Willie Mays, his rookie card looks like a real buy, and it's got nowhere to go but up.

Another hot property, Don Mattingly's 1984 Donruss rookie card had a hand in starting the mid-80s rookie card boom.

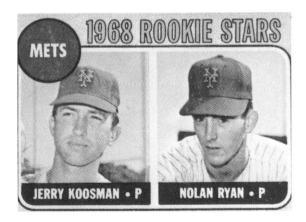

As far as baseball in the 1960s goes, this is *the* card: two of the best pitchers of the 70s and 80s making their first appearances, on the same card and in New York uniforms.

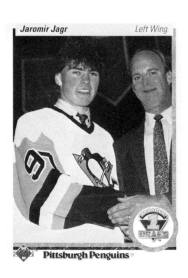

Brett Hull (above) and the
rookie card of Jaromir Jagr
(right) are two reasons for the
popularity of the 1990-91
Upper Deck hockey set.

Going back about 40 years, Robert
"Ted" Lindsay is a popular HOFer,
and this 1951-52 Parkie card is a
strong investment.

Jim Thorpe (right) is one of the key cards in the 1955 Topps All-American set.

This signed Paul Ronty card, from Parkhurst's 1952-53 set, is one of the more popular early hockey cards.

It's up, it's down, but usually it's up: the 1952 Topps Mickey Mantle card, mistakenly viewed by some as his rookie card. You want this card if you can pay a reasonable price for it.

The 1954-55 Topps set, which includes these Dineen (above) and McKenney (right) cards, is Topps' first hockey set and one of the most colorful and popular ever.

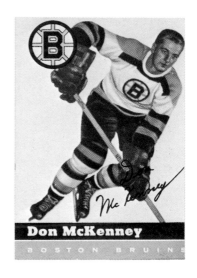

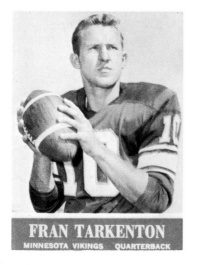

Rookie cards of HOF quarterbacks, like Fran Tarkenton (left) and Don Meredith (opposite, middle), are solid buys if in near-mint or better condition.

If you can find a problem-free rookie card of Jim Brown (right), best running back of all time, buy it even though it goes for $450 at guide value.

JIM BROWN
CLEVELAND BROWNS   FULLBACK

DON MEREDITH
DALLAS COWBOYS   QUARTERBACK   NFL

You can't go wrong with a good-quality rookie card of a household basketball name such as Wilt Chamberlain (right). Just use a little common sense in evaluating the card's price and quality.

LAKERS
WILT CHAMBERLAIN CENTER

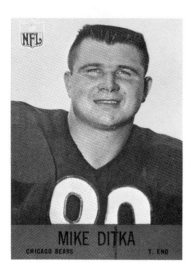

Mike Ditka's rookie card is obviously one with profit potential.

Bart Starr is another HOFer with strong possibilities.

DAVID ROBINSON

Like Wilt Chamberlain's, rookie cards of the likes of Magic Johnson (opposite, bottom), Jordan, Abdul-Jabbar and Robinson are sure winners, provided you use your head when you buy.

Larry Johnson of the Hornets is one of today's young players whose cards have good upside potential.

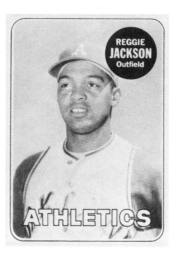

Reggie Jackson's rookie card (above right), about the only one to show him without his trademark brashness, isn't a bad buy even with its several-hundred-dollar price tag. But cards need not be great investments to be fun--witness a real character like Jay Johnstone (above left).

Vander Meer and #167 Preacher Roe. There is good value for the money buying the cheap star cards.

Sell all cards in less than near mint condition.

1951 BOWMAN

This was Bowman's first year of going to a little larger-sized card. This set contains three of baseball's all-time best players' rookie cards: Mickey Mantle, Willie Mays and Whitey Ford. They represent over half the value of this entire set. But instead of buying the entire set, I'd be chasing after the following cards.

BEST BETS:
#1 Whitey Ford
#2 Yogi Berra
#3 Robin Roberts
#30 Bob Feller
#31 Roy Campanella
#32 Duke Snider
#46 George Kell
#50 Johnny Mize
#53 Bob Lemon
#58 Enos Slaughter
#78 Early Wynn
#122 Joe Garagiola
#127 Sal Maglie
#134 Warren Spahn
#165 Ted Williams
#198 Monte Irvin
#232 Nellie Fox
#233 Leo Durocher
#253 Mickey Mantle
#254 Jackie Jensen
#305 Willie Mays
#324 Johnny Pramesa (mint only)

The low number cards #1-#36 in nm/mt or better are also very tough in this grade and would be worth purchasing if you can find them nice.

Sell all cards in less than near mint condition.

1952 BOWMAN

This set doesn't contain any key rookie cards but has some desirable cards nonetheless. Like in 1951 the low number cards #1-#36 in nm/mt condition would be worth acquiring.

BEST BETS:
#1 Yogi Berra
#4 Robin Roberts
#5 Minnie Minoso
#11 Ralph Kiner
#21 Nellie Fox
#30 Red Schoendienst
#43 Bob Feller
#44 Roy Campanella
#75 George Kell
#101 Mickey Mantle
#116 Duke Snider
#142 Early Wynn
#156 Warren Spahn
#196 Stan Musial
#218 Willie Mays
#232 Enos Slaughter
#252 Frank Crosetti (mint only)

Buy all cards in near mint or better condition only.
Sell all cards in less than strict near mint condition.

1953 BOWMAN (COLOR)

Easily one of the most gorgeous card sets produced of all time and thus has become a popular set with collectors. This was Bowman's first effort at the larger-sized cards, probably to compete with

Topps coming out with large cards in 1952. Purchase only cards in near mint condition or better.

BEST BETS:
#1 Davey Williams (mint only)
#18 Nellie Fox
#32 Stan Musial
#33 Pee Wee Reese
#44 Bauer/Berra/Mantle
#46 Roy Campanella
#51 Monte Irvin
#55 Leo Durocher
#59 Mickey Mantle
#65 Robin Roberts
#80 Ralph Kiner
#93 Rizzuto/Martin
#97 Eddie Mathews
#99 Warren Spahn
#114 Bob Feller
#117 Duke Snider
#118 Billy Martin
#121 Yogi Berra
#146 Early Wynn
#153 Whitey Ford

Sell all cards in less than strict near mint condition.

1953 BOWMAN (BLACK AND WHITE)
Bowman decided to do two sets this year, and like their color set, this is one of the nicest black and white sets we have today. This set is very scarce and underrated by most collectors and investors. It's very hard to find in top grades, even the common cards.

BEST BETS:
#15 Johnny Mize
#27 Bob Lemon
#28 Hoyt Wilhelm

#39 Casey Stengel
#52 Ralph Branca

Also I would try and buy any other card from this set if nm/mt or better.

Sell all cards in less than strict near mint condition.

1954 BOWMAN

It would be hard to top the '53 color set but this set is still a nice issue. Most cards from this set are still reasonably priced and one should definitely try and buy a few cards from this set. Buy all cards in strict near mint or better condition only.

BEST BETS:
#1 Phil Rizzuto
#6 Nellie Fox
#23 Harvey Kuenn
#45 Ralph Kiner
#50 George Kell
#57 Hoyt Wilhelm
#62 Enos Slaughter
#64 Eddie Mathews
#65 Mickey Mantle
#66 Ted Williams
#89 Willie Mays
#90 Roy Campanella
#101 Don Larsen
#110 Red Schoendienst
#132 Bob Feller
#161 Yogi Berra
#164 Early Wynn
#170 Duke Snider
#177 Whitey Ford
#196 Bob Lemon
#224 Bill Bruton (mint only)

Sell all cards in less than strict near mint condition.

1955 BOWMAN

This was the last issue produced by Bowman because after the end of the year Topps bought out Bowman for $200,000. This started a virtual monopoly for Topps which resulted in a mediocre run of card production down the road for collectors to buy. This issue, which resembled a television screen, gets mixed feelings from collectors but if you're an investor I would urge you to purchase cards from this issue. They are truly gorgeous in top grades and difficult to find in high grades, which is true for most issues of this era, but especially for this card set.

Buy only cards in strict near mint or better condition.

BEST BETS:
#1 Hoyt Wilhelm
#22 Roy Campanella
#23 Al Kaline
#38 Early Wynn
#59 Whitey Ford
#68 Elston Howard
#103 Eddie Mathews
#134 Bob Feller
#168 Yogi Berra
#171 Robin Roberts
#179 Hank Aaron
#184 Willie Mays
#202 Mickey Mantle
#242 Ernie Banks
#320 George Susce (mint only)

I would in addition look to buy the umpire cards from this set, any of them. I think they are much scarcer in high grades since kids didn't find them popular and didn't save them.

Cards from this set are worth paying a premium to get them in mint condition.

Sell all cards in less than near mint condition.

1951 TOPPS (REDBACKS)

This small card set has been hindered pricewise by a hoard of cases that surfaced many years ago. No one has been able to determine how many cases did show up but as a result 1951 redback packs are still available and reasonably priced. Due to the overabundance of packs, most seem to have been opened up thus these cards are available in top grades without a great deal of difficulty. These cards would be best purchased for long-term hold only.

BEST BETS:
#1 Yogi Berra
#8 Early Wynn
#20 Dom DiMaggio
#22 Bob Feller
#30 Warren Spahn
#36 Gus Zernial (Chicago)
#38 Duke Snider
#50 Monte Irvin
#52 Tommy Holmes (Boston)

Buy only in near mint to mint condition or better.
Sell all cards in less than nm/mt condition.

1951 TOPPS (BLUEBACKS)

As easy as the redbacks are to find, the bluebacks are much scarcer. Even though a blueback variety sells for five times as much as a redback, I definitely think they are still undervalued, very undervalued in fact. A few bluebacks were found in the hoard with the redbacks, but very few packs have come into the marketplace. These cards should do well down the road in high grades.

BEST BETS:
#2 Richie Ashburn
#6 Red Schoendienst
#30 Enos Slaughter
#37 Bobby Doerr
#50 Johnny Mize

I would even try and buy mint commons from this set.
Sell all cards in less than nm/mt condition.

1952 TOPPS

This was Topps' first major card issue and is the key post WWII card issue to date. This set in top grades is wholesaling for over $100,000 and several collectors are asking upwards of $200,000 for their sets. The most expensive card of the era is from this set, that being the #311 Mickey Mantle card. This card has been sold for as high as $75,000 in mint condition. In addition to the Mantle, the first and last cards have brought prices of $20,000 each. Card #1 is Andy Pafko. The reason for the high price is that this card is scarce in mint and centered condition. Card #407 Eddie Mathews is again a condition rarity being the last card in the set and it's a rookie card as well as a high number. All add up to big prices in top grade.

Right now 1952 Topps cards are very popular due to several hoards of packs which were found lately. Thus prices on these cards in mint condition are bringing many times guide. Long term these cards should do very well, especially for gem quality specimens.

BEST BETS:
#2 Pete Runnels (mint only)
#20 Billy Loes (mint only)
#26 Monte Irvin
#33 Warren Spahn
#37 Duke Snider
#48 Joe Page (error)
#49 Johnny Sain (error)
#65 Enos Slaughter
#88 Bob Feller
#91 Red Schoendienst
#129 Johnny Mize
#175 Billy Martin
#191 Yogi Berra
#195 Minnie Minoso

#246 George Kell
#261 Willie Mays
#268 Bob Lemon
#277 Early Wynn
#312 Jackie Robinson
#314 Roy Campanella
#315 Leo Durocher
#392 Hoyt Wilhelm
#406 Joe Nuxhall
#407 Eddie Mathews

The #1 Pafko and #311 Mantle are rather pricey at the moment and I think would be best avoided by most investors at this time. I think mint commons would be a wise purchase at this time, especially the #311–407 high number series. I would try and buy 1952's in nm/mt or better condition.

Sell all cards in less than strict near mint condition.

1953 TOPPS

A very popular set and one scarce in nm/mt condition or better. I would buy only cards in strict near mint condition or better. Always check to make sure the borders haven't been touched up with a red or black marking pen, which is starting to become a common practice by some unscrupulous dealers and some collectors. The prices on cards in this set are still reasonable for their scarcity. A superb long-term buy if I ever saw one.

BEST BETS:
#1   Jackie Robinson
#10 Smokey Burgess
#27 Roy Campanella
#37 Eddie Mathews
#41 Enos Slaughter
#44 Ellis Kinder
#54 Bob Feller
#61 Early Wynn
#72 Fred Hutchinson
#81 Joe Black

#82 Mickey Mantle
#104 Yogi Berra
#119 Johnny Sain
#147 Warren Spahn
#151 Hoyt Wilhelm
#207 Whitey Ford
#220 Satchel Paige
#244 Willie Mays
#280 Milt Bolling (mint only)

I would try and acquire commons from this year as well. Both low and high numbers are worth the money.

Sell all cards in less than strict near mint condition.

1954 TOPPS

This was a great set for key rookie cards. The first cards of players such as Ernie Banks, Al Kaline and Hank Aaron came out of this year's set.

BEST BETS:
#1 Ted Williams
#10 Jackie Robinson
#20 Warren Spahn
#30 Eddie Mathews
#32 Duke Snider
#36 Hoyt Wilhelm
#37 Whitey Ford
#50 Yogi Berra
#90 Willie Mays
#94 Ernie Banks
#128 Hank Aaron
#201 Al Kaline
#250 Ted Williams

Cards from the series #51-#75 are also an excellent value at current guide values. Only buy strict nm/mt or better. The Hank Aaron card is pretty rare in gem quality. I doubt if there are a dozen in existence today. Thus at current market value of around

$4000, I feel it's a steal. Also card #250 of Ted Williams is much scarcer than his card #1 yet guides list them at about the same price. Always try and get #250 if you can.

Sell all cards in less than strict near mint condition.

1955 TOPPS

This year Topps decided to go to a horizontal format, just like Bowman did. Some of the key cards from this year's set were the rookie cards of Sandy Koufax, Roberto Clemente and Harmon Killebrew.

BEST BETS:
#1 Dusty Rhodes (mint only)
#2 Ted Williams
#4 Al Kaline
#28 Ernie Banks
#31 Warren Spahn
#47 Hank Aaron
#50 Jackie Robinson
#123 Sandy Koufax
#124 Harmon Killebrew
#125 Ken Boyer
#155 Eddie Mathews
#156 Joe Black
#161 Chuck Tanner
#164 Roberto Clemente
#194 Willie Mays
#198 Yogi Berra
#210 Duke Snider

The high number series #161-210 are pretty tough in nm/mt or better grade and would be worth going after.

Buy only cards in near mint or better from this year.

Sell all cards in less than strict near mint condition.

1956 TOPPS

A very popular set and the last year Topps made this large-sized card before converting over to today's standard-sized card.

The set is full of Hall of Famers, but short on key rookie cards except for Luis Aparicio. I would be acquiring nice clean cards from this year. In addition to the star cards you may wish to buy some of the team cards which today collectors need to complete their sets. There are the non-dated issues which are easier to come by and the much more difficult dated cards which are worth buying. Also, two checklists are available for this year's set. You occasionally see them, but not in top grades and unchecked. Scarcer checklists like these in top grades should continue to be popular and on want lists for years to come.

BEST BETS:
#1 William Harridge
#2 Warren Giles
#5 Ted Williams
#8 Walter Alston
#10 Warren Spahn
#15 Ernie Banks
#20 Al Kaline
#30 Jackie Robinson
#31 Hank Aaron
#33 Roberto Clemente
#63 Roger Craig
#69 Chuck Tanner
#79 Sandy Koufax
#101 Roy Campanella
#107 Eddie Mathews
#109 Enos Slaughter
#110 Yogi Berra
#118 Nellie Fox
#120 Richie Ashburn
#125 Minnie Minoso
#130 Willie Mays
#135 Mickey Mantle
#150 Duke Snider
#164 Harmon Killebrew
#165 Red Schoendienst
#180 Robin Roberts

#187 Early Wynn
#194 Monte Irvin
#195 George Kell
#200 Bob Feller
#235 Don Newcombe
#240 Whitey Ford
#255 Bob Lemon
#260 Pee Wee Reese
#292 Luis Aparicio
#307 Hoyt Wilhelm
#340 Mickey McDermott (mint only)

Sell all cards in less than strict near mint condition.

1957 TOPPS

This year's cards were one of Topps' best efforts ever. The cards are very attractive and very popular. In top grades the cards have great eye appeal which adds to the set's popularity. Like the 1956, this set also has checklists—four of them—and most are hard to find and are downright scarce in top grades. Checklist 1/2 is the easiest, 2/3 is the next toughest, 3/4 is thought to be the second toughest one, but I feel it's actually harder to get than the 4/5 checklist which most price guides list as the most valuable one. All are scarce and worth acquiring in unmarked condition. Always carefully examine these cards to make sure the cards haven't been marked in and then erased later on. Avoid cards in this condition. Try and get nicely centered cards, as this is a bad year if you're trying to find centered cards.

A note on centering: If you're trying to purchase only cards that are 50/50 or perfectly centered, you're going to become very frustrated very quickly. A card that is 55/45 or even 60/40 may be as good as it may come normally. So if you're chasing for the elusive 50/50 you may be going after something that doesn't exist. I've seen only one '57 Mantle that was mint and dead centered. That piece was sold for over four times guide three years ago and I'm trying to find another piece like it. So it helps to know about certain years for cards if centering is a problem. If it is, you should allow for this characteristic or keep waiting or just not buy one unless it's what you're looking for. Remember, baseball cards were produced to be sold for a penny to children, not to adults for hundreds of dollars each like they are today. Thus the quality control was pretty much secondary, unlike the far superior product we are seeing produced in the 1990s for a much higher price.

BEST BETS:
#1 Ted Williams
#2 Yogi Berra
#7 Luis Aparicio
#10 Willie Mays
#15 Robin Roberts
#18 Don Drysdale
#20 Hank Aaron
#25 Whitey Ford
#29 Whitey Herzog
#35 Frank Robinson
#40 Early Wynn
#55 Ernie Banks
#78 Roberto Clemente
#90 Warren Spahn
#95 Mickey Mantle
#97 Yankees
#120 Bob Lemon
#125 Al Kaline
#154 Red Schoendienst
#165 Ted Kluszewski
#170 Duke Snider
#203 Hoyt Wilhelm
#210 Roy Campanella
#215 Enos Slaughter
#230 George Kell
#250 Eddie Mathews
#302 Sandy Koufax
#328 Frank Robinson
#400 Dodger Sluggers
#407 Yankee Power Hitters

Sell all cards in less than strict near mint condition.

1958 TOPPS

This set definitely dropped off in quality from the previous year. The paper stock was of poor quality and as a result high grade cards are much harder to come by. As in 1957, off-centered cards are very common. Also this set only has one major rookie card, that of Roger Maris. It also contains the yellow names and team color variations. Unlike today's modern variations which are common in comparison to older variations like these, these are very scarce and much tougher to find than the guide price indicates.

BEST BETS:
#1   Ted Williams
#2   Bob Lemon
#5   Willie Mays
#25 Don Drysdale
#30 Hank Aaron
#40 George Kell
#47 Roger Maris
#52 Roberto Clemente
#70 Al Kaline
#85 Luis Aparicio
#88 Duke Snider
#90 Robin Roberts
#100 Early Wynn
#142 Enos Slaughter
#150 Mickey Mantle
#187 Sandy Koufax
#190 Red Schoendienst
#270 Warren Spahn
#285 Frank Robinson
#288 Harmon Killebrew
#307 Brooks Robinson
#310 Ernie Banks
#320 Whitey Ford
#324 Hoyt Wilhelm
#343 Orlando Cepeda
#370 Yogi Berra

#418 Mantle/Aaron
#420 Vada Pinson
#436 Mays/Snider
#440 Eddie Mathews
#464 Curt Flood
#480 Eddie Mathews
#482 Ernie Banks
#483 Luis Aparicio
#484 Frank Robinson
#494 Warren Spahn

Buy all yellow letter variations in strict near mint condition or better.

Sell all cards in less than strict near mint condition.

1959 TOPPS

Topps' last issue of the decade was an improvement over the 1958 cards, but again there's only one key rookie card—that of Bob Gibson. The high number cards from this set are hard to come by and yet the price doesn't indicate its true scarcity. Price guides don't always tell all you need to know. Go to a few shows. Read hobby papers. See what dealers are asking for their cards. If dealers seem to be way above or way below guide prices on certain issues, that should be an indicator to you that maybe the guide is not totally accurate on a particular card or set. Don't TOTALLY rely on guides. Read, ask questions of fellow collectors, and talk to dealers who are willing to share information. Sadly, some aren't. Obviously, I would avoid someone who wouldn't help me if I were spending my money with them. So should you.

BEST BETS:
#8 Phillies
#10 Mickey Mantle
#20 Duke Snider
#40 Warren Spahn
#50 Willie Mays
#150 Stan Musial
#155 Enos Slaughter

#163 Sandy Koufax
#212 Aaron/Mathews
#260 Early Wynn
#310 Luis Aparicio
#338 Sparky Anderson
#349 Hoyt Wilhelm
#350 Ernie Banks
#352 Robin Roberts
#360 Al Kaline
#380 Hank Aaron
#387 Don Drysdale
#430 Whitey Ford
#435 Frank Robinson
#439 Brooks Robinson
#450 Eddie Mathews
#478 Roberto Clemente
#480 Red Schoendienst
#514 Bob Gibson
#515 Harmon Killebrew
#550 Roy Campanella
#559 Ernie Banks
#560 Luis Aparicio
#562 Al Kaline
#561 Hank Aaron
#563 Willie Mays
#564 Mickey Mantle
#571 Warren Spahn

Sell all cards in less than strict near mint condition.

1960 TOPPS

A very unpopular set for years, but now many of the cards in the set seem to be getting popular as the prices of key star cards and Hall of Famers are still very reasonable in many cases. The key rookie cards from this year are Carl Yastrzemski and Willie Mc-Covey. I would suggest going after the superstar cards from this year as, again, I feel the prices are very reasonable for cards that are over thirty years old. You can pay more for rookie cards from the past two or three years than for a 32-year-old Hall of Famer card. These represent true value, not hype which has taken over the new card market.

The stars cards from the #441-#506 series are much harder to find than most collectors would believe. Also, the All-Star cards in the last series currently represent excellent value. One strategy that works very well, especially for those of you who are on a budget, is to buy a lot of inexpensive cards. If you have $325, don't buy a Yastrzemski rookie. Buy ten or twelve different star cards. Percentagewise you will probably do much better than with one expensive item.

BEST BETS:
#136 Jim Kaat
#210 Harmon Killebrew
#240 Luis Aparicio
#264 Robin Roberts
#335 Red Schoendienst
#420 Eddie Mathews
#445 Warren Spahn
#558 Eddie Mathews
#559 Luis Aparicio
#570 Don Drysdale

Sell all cards in less than strict near mint condition.

1961 TOPPS

This set is probably known most for its high number cards that a few years ago used to be to the hottest high number series around. Today that is not the case as the prices have gotten pretty high. Juan Marichal and Billy Williams are the two key rookies from this set.

Like the 1960 set, many of the stars from this year are not that expensive and, again, compared to some late '80s issues, they are downright bargains for a 31-year-old issue. Most of the Hall of Famers and stars from this year should continue to slowly but surely go up in value down the road.

BEST BETS:
#35 Ron Santo
#80 Harmon Killebrew
#120 Eddie Mathews
#160 Whitey Ford
#200 Warren Spahn
#207 Dodger Southpaws
#260 Don Drysdale
#360 Frank Robinson
#440 Luis Aparicio
#472 Yogi Berra
#506 Willie Davis
#545 Hoyt Wilhelm

Sell all cards in less than strict near mint condition.

1962 TOPPS

A very attractive set featuring a wood grain border which makes this one of the condition rarity sets of the '60s. Centering can be a definite problem in this year's cards so try and buy nicely centered cards when you do purchase any. These cards are tough in nm/mt or better and represent good value for the money currently. The more expensive Hall of Famers like Mantle, Mays and Aaron are solid long term plays. Yet other Hall of Famers like Ford or Kaline seem to be absurdly cheap now. They represent some great buys at current guide levels.

Cards #135-#144 are all Babe Ruth cards. They are about the only reasonably priced cards of the Babe from this era. With the recent Babe Ruth movie, these cards may show a strong surge in interest and that, of course, would translate into much higher prices. These cards are a solid buy now.

This year's cards are hard to find above near mint condition. Yet I would encourage you to try and find nm/mt or mint cards. They will cost you more but they should be better percentagewise than near mint cards and will, more importantly, be easier to sell when you are ready to liquidate your cards.

When buying cards always think about when you're going to sell. Buy not only what's popular today but what will still be popular down the road. Sometimes something that's not popular today can become popular. If you can spot cards like this, your profits will grow even more than normal. That's the problem with buying hot cards or issues. Most hot cards become ice cold eventually and you usually can't give away ice cold cards at any price. Again, look to new card issues and you will see this scenario played over and over. Yet most new card buyers never seem to learn. Don't you learn the hard way.

BEST BETS:
#30 Eddie Mathews
#45 Brooks Robinson
#70 Harmon Killebrew
#100 Warren Spahn
#139 Babe Ruth
#150 Al Kaline
#167 Tim McCarver
#243 Robin Roberts
#310 Whitey Ford
#325 Luis Aparicio
#385 Early Wynn

Sell all cards in less than strict near mint condition.

1963 TOPPS

This set is one of Topps' best efforts from the '60s and, like the 1962 set, is a condition rarity. You will find true mint state cards not easy to find. If you do find them, they won't be cheap.

You have to be careful to examine the border, to make sure that they haven't been touched up with colored marking pens to make them appear to be mint. How you check is to look at the corners that appear to be mint and look for wear. If the card has the full color on the corners but underneath ANY wear shows, the card has been doctored. As soon as these cards show wear the color disappears and white starts appearing.

Years ago I examined a 1963 complete set and every card in the set had been touched up. The guy who bought it never noticed it. You have to look closely. You also have to always deal with people you know and trust. Never forget this!

BEST BETS:
#25 Al Kaline
#108 Hoyt Wilhelm
#125 Robin Roberts
#169 Gaylord Perry
#205 Luis Aparicio
#210 Sandy Koufax
#275 Eddie Mathews
#320 Warren Spahn
#353 Billy Williams
#394 Tim McCarver
#415 Bob Gibson
#440 Juan Marichal
#446 Whitey Ford
#544 Rusty Staub

Also nm/mt Hall of Famers and stars from this year should do better than the rest of the market. Quality cards always outdo mediocre items. Always have, always will.

This set contains the rookie cards of Pete Rose, but at this time his cards do not belong in one's portfolio. No one is buying his cards except for the rookie, and that only if it's in top condition. If they reinstate him, which I feel they will eventually, then I would go out and buy some of his cards. If you want to gamble, you can buy them now before the prices move up, which they will when he becomes eligible for Cooperstown.

Sell all cards in less than strict near mint condition.

1964 TOPPS

This is not one of Topps' more exciting issues. Phil Niekro is the only key rookie card, but Tommy John may be the next Hall of Famer out of this year.

Most mid-60s star cards are priced at levels where you can buy them now and hold them for a nice profit down the road. Look for value when buying cards for investment. Don't let hype affect your thinking.

I see an interesting trend starting. Many new investors who got into the card market in the last year or two are now trying to sell all the new cards they purchased recently as they are seeing the folly of their ways and they are finding out new cards aren't a guaranteed way to riches like so many thought. Now they are selling out (some at substantial losses), and they are taking those proceeds and putting them back into older cards. Now if they had only done that in the first place, they would have been much further ahead in the game.

My point is if a lot of money starts leaving new cards for older cards many of these cheaper '60s cards won't stay cheap for very long.

Also I'm starting to hear of more and more Japanese money coming into the card market. Most of it is still small amounts, but that could change very rapidly and without notice. It wouldn't take much serious money to make any one segment of the card market make quick upward moves.

BEST BETS:
#13 Hoyt Wilhelm
#35 Eddie Mathews
#116 Tony Oliva
#120 Don Drysdale
#167 Lou Pinella
#175 Billy Williams
#177 Harmon Killebrew
#230 Brooks Robinson
#244 Tony LaRussa
#260 Frank Robinson
#280 Juan Marichal
#285 Robin Roberts
#287 Tony Conigliaro
#380 Whitey Ford
#400 Warren Spahn
#460 Bob Gibson
#540 Luis Aparicio

Sell all cards in less than strict near mint condition.

1965 TOPPS

This set features the rookie cards of such stars as Steve Carlton, Catfish Hunter, Tony Perez and Joe Morgan.

BEST BETS:
#15 Robin Roberts
#50 Juan Marichal
#176 Willie McCovey
#205 Warren Spahn
#236 Denny McLain
#260 Don Drysdale
#276 Hoyt Wilhelm
#330 Whitey Ford
#400 Harmon Killebrew
#410 Luis Aparicio
#510 Ernie Banks
#581 Tony Perez

Sell all cards in less than strict near mint condition.

1966 TOPPS

Not one of the most exciting looking issues of the decade, but it does have such rookie cards as Jim Palmer, Ferguson Jenkins and Don Sutton. Many cards in the set are hard to find in high grades and the #523-#598 series cards are popular and expensive, especially the star cards and the single print numbers.

BEST BETS:
#1 Willie Mays (mint only)
#36 Catfish Hunter
#90 Luis Aparicio
#110 Ernie Banks
#120 Harmon Killebrew
#125 Lou Brock
#200 Eddie Mathews
#288 Don Sutton
#430 Don Drysdale

#510 Hoyt Wilhelm
#540 Denny McLain

Sell all cards in less than strict near mint condition.

1967 TOPPS

A very attractive and popular '60s issue that contains two of the most popular rookie cards of the era, those of Tom Seaver and Rod Carew. The set contains a very expensive and desirable high number series, #534-#609. The fact that Seaver and Carew were in this last series makes their cards much more expensive than if they were in any other series. Also, the Seaver is a single print versus a double print for the Carew, thus the Seaver is twice as scarce, hence the higher price.

BEST BETS:
#5 Whitey Ford
#55 Don Drysdale
#60 Luis Aparicio
#166 Eddie Mathews
#315 Billy Williams
#422 Hoyt Wilhelm
#460 Harmon Killebrew
#536 Joe Niekro

Sell all cards in less than strict near mint condition.

1968 TOPPS

This is not a tough set, but because of the wood grain borders, it's hard to find in nm/mt or mint condition. This set is also the set where you will find the rookie cards of Nolan Ryan and Johnny Bench which represent almost half the value of the entire set in just these two cards. The Ryan card currently is only a buy in nm/mt or mint and for long term as the card is trading for $1,500-$2,500 in these grades. Make sure to buy one that is centered.

To check 1968 cards for wear, check the reverse first. You can spot wear much easier on the back than the front due to the fact that color can fool the naked eye. Or you can use a magnifying glass.

Most of the key cards are currently good buys for the long term. NM/MT or better cards should do the best.

BEST BETS:
#40 Denny McLain
#58 Eddie Mathews
#80 Rod Carew
#130 Tony Perez
#144 Joe Morgan
#145 Don Drysdale
#205 Juan Marichal
#290 Willie McCovey
#310 Luis Aparicio
#350 Hoyt Wilhelm
#355 Ernie Banks
#408 Steve Carlton
#410 Fergie Jenkins
#450 Jim Kaat
#520 Lou Brock

Sell all cards in less than strict near mint condition.

1969 TOPPS
The last set of the decade features the rookie cards of future HOF'er Reggie Jackson and Rollie Fingers, as well as the last card of Mickey Mantle.

BEST BETS:
#99 Graig Nettles
#200 Bob Gibson
#260 Reggie Jackson
#370 Juan Marichal
#400 Don Drysdale
#510 Rod Carew
#545 Willie Stargell

#565 Hoyt Wilhelm
#640 Fergie Jenkins

Sell all cards in less than strict near mint condition.

1970 TOPPS

The only rookie card in this set of any value is the Thurman Munson card and he's not going to Cooperstown. The cards from this year are hard to find in nm/mt or mint condition. Thus nice clean cards can command premiums when they surface.

BEST BETS:
#17 Hoyt Wilhelm
#140 Reggie Jackson
#150 Harmon Killebrew
#220 Steve Carlton
#230 Brooks Robinson
#250 Willie McCovey
#315 Luis Aparicio
#330 Lou Brock
#380 Tony Perez
#530 Bob Gibson
#537 Joe Morgan
#622 Don Sutton

Sell all cards in less than strict near mint condition.

1971 TOPPS

A very nice and attractive set that is well known in collecting circles for its scarcity in mint condition due to its black borders showing wear very easily. The problem with this set is that some people will take a black marking pen and color in the borders to make them appear to be mint. Again the key is to look for wear. Some cards have black, mint-appearing corners but underneath wear is obvious. Do not buy such cards regardless of how cheap the price is. That is something you should always remember. If you're buying for investment, you want the best. You're not looking for bargains. If it's not what you want to own, don't buy it even if the price is reasonable. Pay a little more and get what you know you should be buying. Don't buy a card that is "close" or with a "minor problem." Pay more, but get more. Let collectors buy the other cards.

The key rookies from this set are Steve Garvey and Bert Blyleven. Long term probably any key star card in this set in nm/mt or mint is probably a good buy as the high-end quality cards keep getting harder and harder to find.

BEST BETS:
#14 Dave Concepcion
#20 Reggie Jackson
#50 Willie McCovey
#117 Ted Simmons
#248 Hoyt Wilhelm
#250 Johnny Bench
#264 Joe Morgan
#361 Don Sutton
#520 Tommy John
#550 Harmon Killebrew
#580 Tony Perez
#600 Willie Mays
#740 Luis Aparicio

Sell all cards in less than strict near mint condition.

1972 TOPPS
A very large and colorful set with only one key rookie card, that of Carlton Fisk. The cards from the last two series can also be a challenge for those putting sets together. The key star cards from this year represent good long-term buys.

BEST BETS:
#51 Harmon Killebrew
#80 Tony Perez
#100 Frank Robinson
#241 Rollie Fingers
#270 Jim Palmer

#280 Willie McCovey
#285 Gaylord Perry
#313 Luis Aparicio
#330 Catfish Hunter
#410 Fergie Jenkins
#420 Steve Carlton
#435 Reggie Jackson
#447 Willie Stargell
#530 Don Sutton
#550 Brooks Robinson
#751 Steve Carlton
#777 Hoyt Wilhelm
    Sell all cards in less than strict near mint condition.

1973 TOPPS

When you think of this set you think of the Mike Schmidt rookie, which is almost half the value of the set by itself. This was also the last year for cards to be issued in series by Topps. The last series, #529-#660, are tough cards and probably much tougher than the guide value indicates. Also the cards were printed on inferior paper and high grade specimens can be hard to find.

BEST BETS:
#10 Don Sutton
#50 Roberto Clemente
#84 Rollie Fingers
#90 Brooks Robinson
#160 Jim Palmer
#165 Luis Aparicio
#170 Harmon Killebrew
#175 Frank Robinson
#180 Fergie Jenkins
#190 Bob Gibson
#199 Bert Blyleven
#230 Joe Morgan
#235 Jim Hunter
#237 Eddie Mathews
#258 Tommy John

#275 Tony Perez
#280 Al Kaline
#300 Steve Carlton
#305 Willie Mays
#370 Willie Stargell

Sell all cards in less than strict near mint condition.

1974 TOPPS

A pretty uninteresting set, to say the least. Not attractive, popular or full of key cards. The Dave Winfield and Dave Parker rookies are the two key cards from this issue as well as the second Mike Schmidt card.

But there are some quality star cards that are priced very reasonably and would be worth putting away.

BEST BETS:
#40 Jim Palmer
#61 Luis Aparicio
#85 Joe Morgan
#95 Steve Carlton
#98 Bert Blyleven
#130 Reggie Jackson
#160 Brooks Robinson
#212 Rollie Fingers
#215 Al Kaline
#220 Don Sutton
#230 Tony Perez
#283 Mike Schmidt
#350 Bob Gibson
#400 Harmon Killebrew
#451 Tommy John
#456 Dave Winfield
#542 Rich Gossage
#634 Eddie Mathews

Sell all cards in less than strict near mint condition.

1975 TOPPS

One of the nicer looking '70s sets, similar to the 1963 set with its colorful borders. Like the 1963 Topps, the borders show even the most minute wear; thus mint cards are hard to come by. Make sure when you buy this year's cards that the corners haven't been colored in.

This set features the rookie cards of Robin Yount and George Brett, and both are headed for the Hall of Fame down the road. Most of the star cards from this year are affordable and represent good value for purchase at this time.

BEST BETS:
#21 Rollie Fingers
#30 Bert Blyleven
#50 Brooks Robinson
#60 Fergie Jenkins
#61 Dave Winfield
#70 Mike Schmidt
#80 Carlton Fisk
#185 Steve Carlton
#220 Don Sutton
#223 Robin Yount
#228 George Brett
#230 Catfish Hunter
#300 Reggie Jackson
#370 Tom Seaver
#540 Lou Brock
#554 Rich Gossage
#640 Harmon Killebrew
#660 Hank Aaron

Sell all cards in less than strict near mint condition.

1976 TOPPS

The only key rookie card in this set is the Dennis Eckersley rookie. The key cards from this set should do okay but nothing spectacular. The key is to be selective in what you buy from this year.

BEST BETS:
#19 George Brett
#98 Dennis Eckersley
#316 Robin Yount
#325 Tony Perez
#355 Steve Carlton
#416 Tommy John
#480 Mike Schmidt
#500 Reggie Jackson
#530 Don Sutton
#550 Hank Aaron

Sell all cards in less than strict nm/mt condition.

1977 TOPPS

Another so-so set typical of what Topps produced during most of the '60s and '70s. The key rookie cards are the Andre Dawson and Dale Murphy.

BEST BETS:
#10 Reggie Jackson
#110 Steve Carlton
#128 Tommy John
#140 Mike Schmidt
#144 Bruce Sutter
#523 Rollie Fingers
#525 Dennis Eckersley
#580 George Brett
#620 Don Sutton
#635 Robin Yount
#655 Tony Perez

Sell all cards in less than strict nm/mt condition.

1978 TOPPS

The rookie cards of Eddie Murray and Alan Trammell head up this Topps set. Star cards from the '70s tend to be very reasonable for the most part considering their age. With the insatiable demand for new cards today, the cards from 1975-85 are a good area for bargain hunting. It may not be as exciting as watching a hot rookie go from pennies to dollars quickly, but at least these cards will go up slowly but surely. It's a good area to invest in if you're a conservative type.

BEST BETS:
#36 Eddie Murray
#100 George Brett
#122 Dennis Eckersley
#131 Bert Blyleven
#140 Rollie Fingers
#173 Robin Yount
#200 Reggie Jackson
#310 Don Sutton
#325 Bruce Sutter
#360 Mike Schmidt
#375 Tommy John
#530 Dave Winfield
#540 Steve Carlton
#560 Dave Parker
#707 Molitor/Trammell

Sell all cards in less than strict nm/mt condition.

1979 TOPPS

This was the year the Beckett price guide came out. It seems card production was way up this year and it also seems that this is the first year that many people started putting cases away. As a result cards from this year aren't that hard to find, but there are a few good cards to purchase from this series. Poor centering can be a problem on this year, so try and find nicely centered specimens.

Speaking of centering, when I mention centering I am referring to the front of the cards. Well, if you're sharp, you will also look at the back of the cards. I try and buy cards that are centered on the reverse as well. I'm not as picky on the reverse, but definitely try and avoid cards that are miscut or 90/10 centering on the reverse. If you start looking at the backs of cards, you will find many cards come poorly centered on the reverse.

BEST BETS:
#24 Paul Molitor
#25 Steve Carlton
#40 Dennis Eckersley
#95 Robin Yount
#116 Ozzie Smith
#212 Carney Lansford
#330 George Brett
#358 Allan Trammell
#610 Mike Schmidt
#640 Eddie Murray
#700 Reggie Jackson

Sell all cards in less than nm/mt condition.

1980 TOPPS

This is where you find the Rickey Henderson rookie card which is almost 60 percent of the entire set's value. Some of the future Hall of Famers are the best buys since they are so cheap.

BEST BETS:
#265 Robin Yount
#270 Mike Schmidt
#393 Ozzie Smith
#450 George Brett
#600 Reggie Jackson

Sell all cards in less than nm/mt condition.

1981 TOPPS
BEST BETS:
#100 Rod Carew
#210 Jim Palmer
#220 Tom Seaver

#254 Ozzie Smith
#370 Dave Winfield
#400 Reggie Jackson
#456 Jeff Reardon
#515 Robin Yount
#540 Mike Schmidt
#600 Johnny Bench
#630 Steve Carlton
#700 George Brett

Buy only cards in strict mint condition.
Sell all cards in less than strict mint condition.

1981 TOPPS TRADED
BEST BETS:
#761 Rollie Fingers
#816 Tim Raines
#819 Jeff Reardon

Buy only cards in strict mint condition.
Sell all cards in less than strict mint condition.

1982 TOPPS
BEST BETS:
#21 Cal Ripken
#30 Tom Seaver
#200 George Brett
#300 Reggie Jackson
#400 Johnny Bench
#435 Robin Yount
#439 Dave Righetti
#452 Lee Smith
#480 Steve Carlton

Buy only cards in strict mint condition.
Sell all cards in less than strict mint condition.

1982 TOPPS TRADED
BEST BET:
#98T Cal Ripken

    Buy only cards in strict mint condition.
    Sell all cards in less than strict mint condition.

1983 TOPPS
BEST BETS:
#83 Ryne Sandberg
#163 Cal Ripken
#350 Robin Yount
#482 Tony Gwynn
#498 Wade Boggs
#500 Reggie Jackson
#600 George Brett

    Buy only cards in strict mint condition.
    Sell all cards in less than strict mint condition.

1984 TOPPS
BEST BETS:
#30 Wade Boggs
#251 Tony Gwynn
#596 Ryne Sandberg

    Buy only cards in strict mint condition.
    Sell all cards in less than strict mint condition.

1984 TOPPS TRADED
BEST BET:
#42T Dwight Gooden

    Buy only cards in strict mint condition.
    Sell all cards in less than strict mint condition.

1985 TOPPS
BEST BET:
#181 Roger Clemens
#536 Kirby Puckett

Buy only cards in strict mint condition.
Sell all cards in less than strict mint condition.

Mickey Mantle
The King of Baseball Cards

For years the most popular cards in the hobby were those of Mickey Mantle. Frank Thomas is now on the scene but I don't think Mickey has much to fear. The cards of Mr. Mantle are still very highly regarded by collectors and investors alike.

Back in 1987 I wrote a newsletter on why one should be buying all of Mickey Mantle's cards. They shortly took off to the moon. Then they leveled off and even saw prices drop as if there were some profit taking going on. Then for years these cards were very quiet, even in the New York area. Then the Sotheby's auction in New York City took place and a 1952 Topps Mantle card fetched $49,500 at this historic auction. This kind of put Mantle cards back in the public eye. Currently 1950s Mantles seem to be on most want lists. Then, of course, his 1960s should follow suit.

Mantle cards currently are in heavy demand in mint condition. For some reason Mantle cards are difficult to find in mint state. My theory is that Mantle cards were the most popular with kids, so they played with his cards more than with the other players. Thus mint state examples are scarce. Also many of his cards come off-center. This makes nicely centered specimens worth a premium.

The 1950s cards seem to be a good buy for nice returns in the next 18 months. His 1960s cards might be a better buy for any hold period of two years or more.

Either way, ALL portfolios should have some Mantle cards in them. The more the merrier.

Here is a breakdown of all the most actively traded Mantle cards on the market today produced by Bowman and Topps.

1951 BOWMAN #253

The most desirable post-war baseball card, or at least it should be, in my opinion. If Mantle is the king of cards, this card should be the one everyone is desiring. But many don't agree with me and opt for the 1952 Mantle card. If you want to own the rookie card of Mickey Mantle, there is only ONE. This is it! There is no other rookie card of Mantle, regardless of what anyone else tells you. If you could find any other 1951 card, that would qualify. So far, as I stated, this is the only known rookie card.

This card has many things going for it. One, it's a rookie card. It's the only known rookie card. It's part of the scarce high number series. It ranks second as the toughest Mantle card to find in mint condition. I've only seen two cards that I would classify as gem mint specimens. I'm sure there are a few more floating around, but I haven't personally seen them.

The card is usually off-center and usually comes out of focus. It's common to see it with printing lines on the front. Gum stains on the reverse are common as well. Thus a nice clean problem-free specimen is not the norm for this card. The card is not scarce. In top grades it becomes very scarce to downright rare in gem condition.

This card is undervalued in nm/mt grades and above. Most collectors do not understand that this card is a condition rarity in nm/mt or better.

It sells for less than half the price of a 1952 Topps Mantle card. This tells me this card is a bargain at current levels compared to the overpriced 1952 Topps card.

This card should be selling for a premium over the 1952

Topps card and may well down the road. Recently a dealer told me we should see this happen with 18 months. The only reason it isn't is a lack of knowledge by collectors and investors regarding this card's scarcity in top grades. Also the 1952 Topps card has always been a expensive card, and people think just because a card is more expensive that it's rarer. For this card, that is not the case.

If you can afford a card of this value, I would highly encourage purchasing one and putting it away. It will hit six figures one day.

This card is a classic baseball card and one of the best cards to own if you're a serious investor.

Right now sharp mint specimens are fetching $25,000 and will be over $30,000 very soon.

1952 BOWMAN #101

With the 1951 Bowman card taking off, this card is sort of being left in the dust pricewise. If you can afford the 1951, this would be a good alternative.

Back in 1986 we found a small hoard of this card in gem condition. We sold them off for the astounding price then of $260 each. This card can be found in top grades with a little patience. This is sort of the poor man's '51 Mantle, since it is the only other card of the same size as the '51 rookie card.

1953 BOWMAN #59

If you want a superb looking card of the Mick, this might fit the bill. 1953 Bowmans are one of the most attractive sets ever produced. It is also one of the toughest Mantle cards to find in mint state, but worth the wait if you can find such a specimen. Try to find a piece without the reverse gum stain which seems to be common on this card. I used to see this card for sale, but now it seems to have dried up almost totally. Will be hard to find in top grades but a highly recommended card.

The last nice piece I saw sold for $3900 in mint condition.

1954 BOWMAN #65

Probably the least popular card produced by Bowman. But it's still one of the keys to the '54 Bowman set. Top grade specimens do surface from time to time. So wait for a nice piece before you purchase this card.

1955 BOWMAN #202

The last card Bowman produced of Mickey but one of the prettiest in my mind. Many don't like the TV concept, but I see this card in more demand today than ever, especially in top grades. This is the third toughest Mantle card to find in mint state. It is also the most expensive card in the set. This is a definite condition rarity as are all 1955 Bowman cards with their woodgrain borders which show even the most minute wear. When found with full gloss, this card is as gorgeous as they come. Several things you should be looking for when buying this card. Since they are hard to find in mint, some unscrupulous people trim this card. Also I've seen this card reglossed. Check on the back to make sure it is not totally off-center on the reverse. Many '55 Bowmans suffer from this malady. Check the left side of the card. It should show a border. The more the better. I like the potential of this card. If you see anything approaching nm/mt or better, buy it. But don't buy this card from just anyone. Make sure you purchase one from someone who will stand behind the card, because this card is subject to being tampered with.

Several nice mint specimens have sold recently for $1800 each.

1952 TOPPS #311

The most expensive postwar baseball card and I don't understand why. In 1986 a hoard of '55 surfaced in mixed grades, though most were nice. This card is a double print. It's not rare in mint state. The card is difficult to find centered, though. In the recent Sotheby's auction a mint specimen with 70/30 centering brought over $45,000. One New York dealer just sold several pieces for $75,000 each, a record price for this card. I feel this card is currently peaked out and will drop in value this year. A lot of collectors are currently selling this card and taking profits and you can't blame them. You would too if you purchased this card 10 years ago for less than $1,000 and were being offered over 30 times what you paid for it, especially if you're smart and understand what profit taking means.

Short term I don't feel this card is a recommended buy. Long term, maybe, if you can afford to tie up this amount of money.

This is the most famous card of the modern era, but definitely not for most investors' portfolios due to its price and price fluctuations.

1953 TOPPS #82

This is the toughest Mantle card to find in mint condition. Same in gem mint state. Until a recent hoard of 1953s came out of Canada from unopened packs, this card was virtually non-existent in mint condition. Oh yes, I've seen them advertised for years but 99.9% weren't what the ads stated.

This card is selling for way over guide. One mint specimen just went for $6,500. Also one dealer is willing to PAY $10,000 for a gem piece from the Canadian hoard. And just the other day another absolutely stone gem mint specimen surfaced. One dealer allegedly offered $15,000 for the piece, it was that incredible. To find one centered, without the rough cut and with full red border on the bottom, is a tough proposition to say the least.

I highly recommend the purchase of this card, but the price is starting to quickly get out of the range for most buyers. If your wallet can handle this size purchase, go for it. This card is starting to show its merits as a true rarity in gem condition.

1956 TOPPS #135

A very popular card since this was his triple crown year. The key to the '56 set and the last of the large size cards by Topps. This card suffers from poor centering and sometimes comes with print lines on the front of the card. Strict mint specimens are in strong demand with pieces changing hands in the close to $2000 range right now. A good buy for the short or long term.

1957 TOPPS #95

Try and find this card mint and centered. I've only seen one and we sold that for $1700 when they were booking around $550. This is a very attractive card in mint state. Again centering is a major problem with this card. Also check that the card hasn't been re-glossed as they can come glossy and are gorgeous in this condition. As with all Mantle's, in mint this is a wise buy. Short term or long term, buy this card. The past few months I've seen the demand on this card increase dramatically by both collectors and investors. One of the better 1950s cards of the Mick which is being overlooked in my opinion.

1958 TOPPS #150

One of the sleeper cards in mint state. Overlooked by many in gem condition. Usually found off-center. One of the key cards to the '58 set and worth putting one away for a "rainy" day. Top grade specimens are now over $1000, if you can find one.

1959 TOPPS #10

This is the last card made in the decade of the 1950s and the easiest card to find in top grades from this era. Mint specimens are starting to get some big prices. One dealer just sold a mint card for $1300 and I'm sure a year from today that will go much higher. Another card that suffers from centering problems, common for all '59 cards. This card should slowly continue to increase in value.

1959 TOPPS #564

A overlooked card because it's a high number, but a very difficult card to be sure. Ask any collector trying to complete this year's set. Make sure to buy a nicely centered example and you should see nice steady profits down the road.

1960 TOPPS #350

The first Mantle card of this new decade is not one of his most popular cards. Many collectors didn't seem to like the horizontal format very much. The card seems to be available in top grade due to quite a few boxes of cello and wax surfacing over the past few years. Still the key card of the 1960 set and will be a steady performer down the road.

1960 TOPPS #563

This card, like the '59 high number card, is overlooked, but is probably a little tougher than many realize. This card in reality should be selling more than the low number, but demand says the low number is more popular thus it sells for less than it's rarity. Nice high grade pieces can be found with a little patience. Pay a little extra and buy a nice problem-free piece.

1961 TOPPS #300

This is one of the easier Mantle cards to find in mint, but that doesn't mean it's easy to find in mint. I know of several that have sold for four figures recently. Centering is a common problem with this issue, so try and wait for one that is centered decently. Should show continued, if slow, growth down the road.

1961 TOPPS #578

Years ago, '61 high number cards were the rage in the hobby, and this card used to sell like hotcakes. It is still a good buy in top condition. This card can be found in choice grades; it won't be cheap, but at least you can get one if you're willing to pay the price, which can't be said for many Mantle cards. Since cards are cyclical, look for this card to get hot again down the road. One thing to try and avoid is specimens with black printing marks on the front of this particular issue.

1962 TOPPS #200

A true condition rarity, it ranks #6 on our list of the rarest Mantle cards in mint state. In gem condition, you have a long wait trying to find one and when you do, you won't like the price. I saw a gem for sale two years ago for $1800. But no one would bite the bullet and pay that number. Look for nicely centered specimens. Again, make sure it hasn't been reglossed. Check and double check this card before paying for it. This card is commonly trimmed due to the woodgrain border, just like the '55 Bowman issue. This card is not cheap in top grades, thus beware if you see a nice card that is priced "too cheaply." This card should continue to do very well in the next few years. The key will be finding it. But it will be worth the effort when you do find a super piece.

1963 TOPPS #200

A very popular 60s issue. The key to this card is to make sure the corners haven't been colored in with a marking pen. Centering is also important in this issue. Second toughest mint 60's Mantle card and rightly so. A good buy, especially in mint condition. Choice specimens are fetching close to $700 right now.

1964 TOPPS #50

One of the easiest of all Mantle cards to acquire in mint condition. Again, not easy to find, just for this card. Should do above average the next few years. A nice mint specimen will go for around $350 or so currently.

1965 TOPPS #350

This card used to be a sleeper from the '60s. Not any longer. Still the third most difficult card from the '60s and a bear to find centered. In a recent auction this card just went for $1300. This is one of the best cards to acquire from this decade in top grades. Will do very very well down the road. A nice mint specimen is around $650 or so, but one recently sold at auction for over $1000.

1966 TOPPS #50

This is the easiest Mantle card on our list to find in mint state. Not one of the most exciting cards ever made of Mickey, but should do okay the next few years. Just pick up an example that is problem-free which shouldn't be too much of a problem. This card in mint is trading at around $250 currently.

1967 TOPPS #150

Normally a Mantle card is one of the most expensive cards in any set, but not this year due to Carew and Seaver rookies cards in this year's set. Another card not rare in mint state, but centering can be a big problem here. Price hasn't gone out of sight yet, but that could change if Mantle cards run up again like they did in

1987. A mint example of this card will set you back at least $300 today.

1968 TOPPS #280

One of the most inexpensive of all Mantle regular issue cards but all 1968 cards are difficult to find in mint state. If you find a nice card it will exhibit nice gloss and should be a very attractive card. If you're on a budget, this may be the card for you to buy. The going price for this card in mint condition is $300.

1969 TOPPS #500

Usually the last card of a player is his most expensive, but not so with the card of the Mick. This has always been a very popular issue with collectors. Many 1969 vending boxes from this series exist, thus this card in top grades is available and in quantity if you know the right dealer. This card will set you back around $350 in mint condition today.

1969 TOPPS #500A (WHITE LETTER VARIATION)

One of the more popular error cards of the '60s. Back in early 1988 this card was going for $1500-2000 in SCD auctions regularly. Prices have come down quite a bit, but this card is still a tough issue especially in mint state. This may be a excellent time to start buying one or two of these to put away. I don't think anyone has vending boxes of this card. I've seen this card in the $500 range lately, but I anticipate the price to slowly start rising.

RELATIVE RARITY OF MANTLE CARDS IN MINT CONDITION

Which Mantle cards are the hardest to find in mint condition? Which are the easiest? This is our ranking of all 25 Mantle cards we have just discussed. We first did this back in 1987 and there have been changes since then and I'm sure five years from today there will be more adjustments to this chart.

YEAR	COMPANY	CARD NUMBER	RANKING
1951	Bowman	#253	2
1952	Bowman	#101	9

YEAR	COMPANY	CARD NUMBER	RANKING
1953	Bowman	#59	4
1954	Bowman	#65	10
1955	Bowman	#202	3
1952	Topps	#311	11
1953	Topps	#82	1
1956	Topps	#135	8
1957	Topps	#95	7
1958	Topps	#150	5
1959	Topps	#10	12
1959	Topps	#564	16
1960	Topps	#350	19
1960	Topps	#563	18
1961	Topps	#300	17
1961	Topps	#578	15
1962	Topps	#200	6
1963	Topps	#200	13
1964	Topps	#50	24
1965	Topps	#350	14
1966	Topps	#50	25
1967	Topps	#150	22
1968	Topps	#280	20
1969	Topps	#500	23
1969	Topps	#500A	21

If you're buying cards, I can't stress the fact that you should own a few cards of Mr. Mantle. Like him or hate him, his cards are a good buy especially for the long term, because he is the King of Cards.

Future Baseball Hall of Famers

Years ago, the main collector or investor interest was always in proven players, especially the Hall of Famers like Koufax, Killebrew or Spahn. Today we know to make the best returns for your dollar you should be taking a long hard look at purchasing FUTURE Hall of Famers, those who look like they will be going to Cooperstown in the future.

We will help you by giving you my picks for many future baseball Hall of Famers. We will break them down into three categories. DEFINITELY. Those who should make it without any problem unless they pull a Pete Rose type stunt. PROBABLY. Those who either have retired and appear to have the stats to get in, but since you and I don't vote, we have to see what the sportswriters think. Or players who are currently playing and seem to be headed for Cooperstown based on what they have accomplished so far in their careers which would lead one to believe that they are fit company for the Walter Johnson's or the Ty Cobb's of baseball's elite. Our final category will be MAYBE'S. These are guys on the borderline, at least in my opinion. Some from this list will get in eventually. Many will not.

I'm sure you will have fun with this list, agreeing with some choices and disagreeing with others. I'm not saying these players will or will not make it, just what I think the writers will eventually do with their votes. Obviously this is gambling on some players and a sure thing on others. But that is what makes this so fun. It will prove to be very lucrative for many of you if your purchases do indeed go to the Hall some day soon.

DEFINITELY GOING IN

Steve Carlton. 300+ wins, lots of K's. No surprise here.

Nolan Ryan. Again 300+ wins, all-time strikeout leader and #1 no-hit pitcher. Easily will make it on first ballot.

Reggie Jackson. A member of the 500 home run club, all-time great World Series players. Another first ballot member when his time comes.

Carlton Fisk. This catcher was one of the best of his era for sure, yet I hear many say he's only good because he played a long time. Let's see what the writers think.

Mike Schmidt. One of the greatest third basemen of all time? Many think so, and another first ballot inductee when his time comes.

George Brett. His 3000th hit late in 1992 should cement his entry to Cooperstown.

Robin Yount. His 3000th hit after the 1992 All-Star game will help him join Brett in the Hall from the class of 1975 rookie cards.

Ozzie Smith. The Wizard wowed them with his infield play. One of the best and most exciting to watch.

Rickey Henderson. The most exciting leadoff hitter of all time. Trying to put the career stolen base record out of reach, even from Vince Coleman. Has an ego problem, but one of the best.

Cal Ripken, Jr. Is there a manager in the majors who wouldn't have given anything to have this superstar play for his team? A sure first ballot HOF'er.

Wade Boggs. With a lifetime batting average of almost .350, what else is there to say, though his 1992 was terrible.

Tony Gwynn. Doesn't get much press, but just goes out and does a great job year after year.

Ryne Sandberg. The current record holder in salary at 7.1 million per year. At least this guy earns his money. A player that just does his job and does it very very well.

Jeff Reardon. When I first started this list, I had him on the maybe list, now with the record for most saves, a definite.

Dave Winfield. Doesn't look like he will reach the 500 home run club, but will get close and that should be enough to get in the Hall.

PROBABLY WILL MAKE IT IN

Roger Clemens. If he keeps his current pace for a few more years will easily make it to the Hall.

Kirby Puckett. A player that other players should try to emulate. Can't see any reason he wouldn't be enshrined one day soon.

Dwight Gooden. If he can keep his head on straight, his skills should earn him immortality. Might break the career won-lost percentage if Clemens doesn't.

Eddie Murray. Keeps putting up the numbers; don't think he'll hit 500 dingers, but should get in anyways.

Allan Trammell. Many insiders feel he's a sure HOF'er; I think he will get in. Much better player than many realize.

Andre Dawson. A few more years adding to his stats should solidify his chance to enter Cooperstown.

Dennis Eckersley. With Rollie Fingers getting into the Hall, look for more relievers to start joining Fingers and Wilhelm in the Hall. He's one of the best.

Gary Carter. Many mixed feelings on this catcher. Many think he's in for sure, others say no way. I think he will get enshrined.

Dave Parker. Just a few more years and he will probably get his 3000th hit and bingo, Cooperstown, here he comes. Here is another player who many think won't get in.

Bob Boone. This iron man of catchers should impress enough voters with his overall career play to eventually make it in.

Don Sutton. A long career with lots of victories should make enough voters take notice even if not right away.

Tony Perez. Will be inducted. How can they overlook this man's credentials?

Tommy John. Has the numbers to be considered for induction and will make it, even if it takes a little wait.

Sparky Anderson. His managerial skills, not his playing days will get him in.

Pete Rose. Will probably make it because baseball hierarchy doesn't understand the meaning of a lifetime ban. He should be kept out as a lesson to other players not to bet on baseball. His on-the-field skills were as good as they come, but not the kind of role model you want your kids to grow up and follow. Again, baseball will vote him in down the road.

MAYBE WILL MAKE IT IN

Darryl Strawberry. If he keeps up the pace, he should make it in the 500 homer club.

Steve Sax. He keeps putting on some pretty impressive stats very quietly, but don't know if they will be enough to impress the voters when the time to vote him in comes.

Lee Smith. Another of the key relievers of this era, should make it.

Jack Morris. Keeps plugging away, but will he plug away long enough to get any attention from the voters?

Lance Parrish. Has a small chance to get in, but not likely.

Bruce Sutter. Another of the 300 saves club, will this be enough to put him into the HOF?

Dale Murphy. Many think he's going in without any problem. I think it will be a little tougher than that.

Goose Gossage. One of the hardest throwers of all time, another of the 300 saves club. Should be in one day soon.

Dwight Evans. Good solid numbers, but will they be good enough?

Dave Concepcion. It was a pleasure to watch this man play. Hope the voters feel the same way as I do.

Bert Blyleven. Can he win 300 games to assure his entry to Cooperstown or can he make it with his current numbers which are pretty impressive?

Ted Simmons. A long shot to get in, but a pretty fair country player to be sure.

Steve Garvey. I don't think he should get in, but others say yes. Let's see what the voters say.

Lou Piniella. His managing record should get him in, not his playing records.

Ron Santo. A lot of interest in his cards recently which tells me a lot of people are betting he's going to make it in. Let's see who's right.

Jim Kaat. A player who made it through longevity. Some think that's not enough to get in. Let's see what the voters think.

Whitey Herzog. His managerial record may get him in someday.

Tommy LaSorda. Obviously one victory as a pitcher won't cut it, but what a personality and manager to boot. Can that be enough to make Tommy immortal in his lifetime?

Billy Martin. Can the wild career of this man be enough to get him into Cooperstown some day soon?

Dick Williams. Another manager who may be in some day.

Nellie Fox. Like Ron Santo, a lot of collectors are buying his card because they think he's going to get in. Again, let's see what the voters will say, if anything.

I didn't consider any players whose rookie cards came out in 1986 or later. This is an area on which we are still speculating. Players here may have had solid starts in their careers, but to make it to the Hall, you have to play ten years minimum and they have to be outstanding seasons, year after year. The Hall of Fame is not for the mediocre, but the best of the best for a career. Many players come out hot, but fade fast like Ralph Garr. Will Ken Griffey, Jr., keep up his fast start? What about Bo Jackson, remember all the hype on him? Players like Will Clark, Jose Canseco, Cecil Fielder, Ruben Sierra, and Barry Bonds are all top players of our time, but will they keep up their pace? Some will, most won't. Remember, most players will never see the Hall. Keep this in mind when purchasing your cards. Not all your purchases will make it. So be very selective when buying, especially cards from the past five years. This is a very risky area. But of course, the rewards can be big IF you can pick the winners.

Future Hall of Famers should be a part of everyone's investment portfolio. They will prove to be solid performers down the road.

Football Cards

A few years ago very few people were buying football cards outside of a few diehard collectors. Football card collecting has grown tremendously the past three years. Also investors realized the great potential in football cards and the value of these cards has indeed increased dramatically, yet there are good deals still left out there. Here are a few of the best tips I see for football cards. Buy only cards in near mint or better for cards before 1980. Cards after 1980 try to buy in mint only.

1956 Topps #71 Stan Jones rookie. Just made it into the Hall but his rookie card is only $12. Could be a good buy down the road if you're buying at this reasonable price.

1956 Topps #101 Roosevelt Grier rookie. At only $26, we have a definite card to buy today. Too cheap in my mind for a card of this caliber and this era.

1956 Topps #41 Roosevelt Brown rookie. $32 for this HOF'er. Less than an Emmitt Smith rookie who is a long ways from the HOF. Some good buys in older cards like this if you hunt around.

1956 Topps Checklist. Guide value is $300 but far scarcer than the price indicates. Try and find a nice nm/mt or mint specimen that is unchecked. Great long term item for this scarce card.

1957 Topps Checklist. This card lists for $400 but is much scarcer than the '56 checklist. I've seen ones that were in vg condition and marked with asking prices of $500 or more. This is a very undervalued card and a steal at anywhere near guide value. I would buy this card, even if you had to pay a premium.

1958 Topps #62 Jim Brown rookie. The best running back of all time. Thus very popular and currently guide value is $450, but the key is to find a clean problem-free card. You should try and find one that is centered and one with the photo in focus. This will be hard to find but will be worth the effort. Great long term card and undervalued in high grades.

1960 Fleer #7 Sid Gillman rookie. A Hall of Famer card for $9. I'd buy some at this giveaway price.

1961 Topps #182 Jim Otto rookie. A HOF'er and just $30. Not bad for a 31-year-old card.

1963 Topps #95 Willie Wood rookie. Another HOF'er card that's on the move and up to $30, but still has enough momentum to keep it moving up more.

1963 Topps #155 Larry Wilson rookie. A 30-year-old HOF'er card at $20. Should start moving once people wake up to this card and others from this era at these type of reasonable prices.

1964 Topps #90 Bobby Bell rookie. A Hall of Famer and just $25 right now. I'd buy one or two at this price level.

1964 Topps #92 Buck Buchanan rookie. A HOF'er and just $25, worth picking up several pieces.

1965 Philadelphia #195 Charlie Taylor rookie. A HOF'er at $40, but a great one. Room to move here for sure.

1965 Topps #137 Ben Davidson rookie. A tough single print from this very popular football set. Up to $30 but more room left for price to rise in the next few years.

1970 Topps #59 Alan Page rookie. At $14 for a rookie card of a HOF'er, seems like someone is overlooking this all-time great. You can buy a proven performer or invest in a new card at the same price level who will get into Canton only if he pays the admission at the front door. Buy value, not HYPE. You have value here.

1970 Topps #247 Fred Dryer rookie. Up to $16, but more room left to move.

1970 Topps #75 Lem Barney rookie. Current book value is $2.50. This card is a steal at this level. It can easily go to $10+. Buy them now.

1971 Topps #257 Mark Moseley rookie. At $5 looks like one of the bargains from this year's cards. Pick up a half dozen of this card.

1971 Topps #113 Ken Houston rookie. Just $16 for this HOF'ers rookie card. A good deal if you ask me.

1971 Topps #114 Willie Lanier rookie. Again a HOF'er at just $15, buy a few today.

1972 Topps #101 L.C. Greenwood rookie. At $12 you have to go out and buy a few of this standout. Up 50% in the past year and not done moving up.

1972 Topps #65 Jim Plunkett rookie. At $20 a good buy. Can easily double without much trouble.

1972 Topps #186 Gene Upshaw rookie. A HOF'er and just $15. Sounds like a good play for the money.

1972 Topps #244 Charlie Joiner rookie. This card went up 50 percent over the past year to $18 and also is on the move. A future Hall of Famer for sure. But not many seem to know this, thus pick up some second or third year cards as well. When a player makes it into the Hall, ALL his cards go up in value. Actually the cheapest cards tend to go up the highest percentagewise, so this may be an angle for those of you who are on a budget and want more bang for your buck.

1972 Topps #106 Lyle Alzado rookie. At $14 a solid buy. Should be inducted into Canton one day soon. Buy them before the masses do.

1973 Topps #288 Jack Tatum rookie. This card is up 100 percent the past year to $2.50. One of the most ferocious hitters of all time, worth a fling at this extremely favorable price.

1973 Topps #343 Jack Youngblood rookie. Up 50 percent the past year to $10, but too cheap for such a talented player. I'd buy one or two of this card.

1973 Topps #115 Jack Ham rookie. This HOF'ers cards have been quiet till the past year when it doubled. But even at $20 it still has room to go up quite a bit more.

1973 Topps #34 Ken Anderson rookie. If you check the top 20 statistics for quarterbacks, his name is plastered all over the record books. Yet his card is quiet at $20, but should awaken one day and then it will go up and fast.

1974 Topps #219 Ray Guy rookie. One of the greatest punters of all-time. Guide value is $6, buy a small group for this future Hall of Famer.

1974 Topps #121 Harold Carmichael rookie. This card was $4 last year, now it's up to $9 for this future HOF'er. Pick some up today.

1975 Topps #367 Dan Fouts rookie. Headed for the HOF. At $60 right now, but should hit $100+ without any problem very soon.

1975 Topps #12 Mel Blount rookie. Here is a rookie card of a Hall of Famer that is way too reasonable. That tells me it's time to buy up a few. You can't lose, so let's get several pieces soon.

1975 Topps #282 Lynn Swann rookie. Put this Steeler receiver down for Canton in the very near future. His card is only $29, so we have a chance to make some nice money here.

1976 Topps #158 Randy White rookie. A future Hall of Famer. $18 now, but will go up much higher. All cards of players who go to Canton go up in value. To maximize your profits, you buy them before they go in and before the masses start buying.

1976 Topps #427 Ed "Too Tall" Jones rookie. This card is up 50 percent in the past year, so someone is chasing after this card. At $10 and seems like a buy at that level.

1976 Topps #34 Pat Leahy rookie. Looking for a bargain? I checked several guides and they list this card as a common. The oldest player in the NFL, so he must be doing something right. Again, at this price buy up a quantity. Zero downside.

1977 Topps #99 Mike Webster rookie. A future Hall of Famer and just $4 right now. Buy them pronto!

1977 Topps #146 Harry Carson rookie. At $5 this card is one of the best kept secrets in football card collecting. Plays in a media town, but may be headed for Canton and watch his cards go up then. Key is to buy today, before everyone else realizes this fact.

1978 Topps #315 Tony Dorsett rookie. Guide value is $35 and dropping currently. I would be aggressively buying this card for long term hold. Too cheap for a player of this quality.

1978 #320 John Stallworth rookie. This card doubled in the past year, which is starting to tell me someone is wise to the fact that Mr. Stallworth is a future HOF'er. His second and third year cards should be easy to get reasonably priced right now.

1979 Topps #310 James Lofton rookie. This card is up more than double in the past year since everyone recently woke up to this man's super stats as a receiver. At $35 not a sleeper but a future Canton resident which should drive his cards up even more. Try and find cards which are centered which will be very hard in this issue. Also try and buy a few '80 and '81 cards of Mr. Lofton as well.

1979 Topps #390 Earl Campbell rookie. Just made it into the Hall of Fame, but still an excellent buy. Ones that are mint and centered are hard to come by, also they are not available in quantity for a card that isn't that old yet.

1979 Topps #308 Ozzie Newsome rookie. A hard card to find in nice shape. Up to $24 but headed for Canton down the road. So pick up a few '80 and '81 cards as well. You won't be able to pick up the rookie in quantity, so buy what you can find.

1980 Topps #170 Ottis Anderson rookie. Another running back who hit 10,000+ yard rushing recently and headed for the HOF. Card is at $13 right now and soft, so a good time to pick a few of this solid card.

1981 Topps #194 Art Monk rookie. One of the all-time great receivers. Guaranteed to end up in the Hall of Fame soon after he retires. Card is up to $50, but will continue to go up year after year. Also buy up some '82 and '83 cards as well.

1981 Topps #216 Joe Montana rookie. When you talk about the best of the best, this quarterback has to be mentioned. This card's prices have been as high as $350 and now are down to around $140 in the price guides. Yet I have actually seen them for sale even below that price. This card is a definite buy at current market value. If you buy this, only buy mint and centered specimens. Again, if you are offered these cards off-center or less than mint, pass. Buy quality even if you have to pay a premium.

1981 Topps #150 Kellen Winslow rookie. Another future HOF'er, but a sleeper in my mind as not many investors are looking for the card. Up about 100 percent in the past year, now at $5. Buy 20 pieces, it will make you some nice profits.

1981 Topps #316 Dan Hampton rookie. Up 50 percent in the past year to its current price of $10. Should continue going up the next few years.

1981 Topps #213 Nick Lowery rookie. Many guides list this card as a common. Obviously their price consultants haven't watched a football game in the past decade. At less than a buck, an absolute steal. One of the best and most consistent kickers of all-time. Buy all you can, NOW! Even get '82 and '83 cards, but you'll have to dig them out of commons boxes as well, unless your dealer hasn't thrown them away yet.

1982 Topps #434 Lawrence Taylor rookie. One of the most exciting defense players of his era and quite popular with collectors as well. Up to $40 right now, but a very quiet card, so a great time to buy. Going to the HOF so now is the time to buy. Pick up some of his '83 and '84 cards as well.

1982 Topps #486 Ronnie Lott rookie. This card shot up this past season as many thought he was all washed up. An obvious future Hall of Famer, not a bargain at $30 but will continue to increase in value. Definitely pick up some '83 and '84 cards of Mr. Lott as well, as they are much cheaper and will go up in value as well.

1982 Topps #51 Anthony Munoz rookie. One of the best at his position of all-time. At $8 a steal, because most fans never watch offensive lineman play. Headed for Canton. Buy his '83 and '84 cards as well. Zero downside! Nuff said.

1981 JOGO (CFL) Warren Moon rookie. This was the first card issued for this great quarterback. This black and white over-sized postcard type card is very scarce. About 1000 sets were produced but you never see them for sale. Also you see the 1983 JOGO card advertised as his rookie, but that of course is his second card. Dealers are asking anywhere from $750 to $1500 for that card. What is this card worth? I can't quote you one actual sale price because I haven't seen or heard of any actual sales. I know I sold eight complete sets back in the early '80s for $20 a set. If the '83 card is selling for $750 and up, this card has to be worth a 50% premium above that. With Mr. Moon showing the world he is one of the best, his early cards like this should become increasingly more popular. Also I know I have been offered the 1983 card in quantities of 25 pieces for $500 each wholesale. 1983's are available, the 1981's are rare.

1983 Topps #38 Mike Singletary rookie. We recommended this card at $4 last year, now it's up to $8 and it's not even close to the top. A guaranteed future Hall of Famer, so buy up some '84 and '85 cards as well. Can't miss, unless you don't buy any now.

1983 Topps #294 Marcus Allen rookie. One of the all-time great Raider running backs, but his cards aren't priced accordingly. Looks like a good buy here. Also pick up some '84 and '85 cards as well at $2 and 75 cents respectively.

1983 Topps #25 Gerald Riggs rookie. Been overlooked for a long time, but showed some glitter in the last Super Bowl. Up to $2, but should move quite a bit more the next few years. Much better than the price of the card indicates.

1984 Topps #380 Darrell Green rookie. We recommended this card recently at 75 cents, now it's up to $2 as fans are waking up to his superb abilities. Still an excellent value.

1984 Topps USFL #58 Reggie White rookie. A great player from this limited production set. Guide is $35 but try and find them. Potential to $100+

1984 USFL #52 Steve Young rookie. Proved that he is more than a bench warmer as a quarterback. $30, but still a good value, scarce and in demand.

1984 Topps #300 Morten Anderson rookie. A good solid player, yet his card is a steal at $1.25. I'd buy a hundred or so of this card.

1984 Topps #286 Jackie Slater rookie. Guide price is 45 cents. Stock up with a few hundred. This quality card for pennies is a steal.

1984 Topps #123 Dan Marino rookie. One of the best in the game today and the key card to this set. The card isn't cheap at $60, but compare it to a Joe Montana card. Obviously Super Bowl rings mean something to the value of football cards. All football portfolios should have several of this card in it. On a more expensive card like this for those of you on a budget, take a look at a second year card or even a third year card of a guaranteed future Hall of Famer. Sometimes they outperform rookie cards since they a more reasonably priced. But the best strategy is to get a few of each. Diversification is one of the keys to maximizing your profit potential in the card market.

IMPORTANT POINT: Football cards were printed in much smaller quantities than baseball cards from the same era. One dealer who specializes in football cards told me that he felt that early 1980s football cards were printed in quantities that were maybe 5 percent or 10 percent of baseball cards from the same era. If these figures are anywhere near the truth, then some of the pre-1985 cards might represent excellent value for the money.

1985 Topps #24 Richard Dent rookie. Up 50 percent in the past year and still a deal at $6. Pick up a dozen or so.

1985 Topps #251 Warren Moon. His first Topps card and hard to find in mint condition. Also look for some of his '86 cards as well.

1985 Topps #111 Carl Banks rookie. A top quality player, yet only $3. A good play for the price.

1986 Topps #255 Boomer Esiason rookie. A good player, but his card is only $8 and definitely has room to go up 100 percent or more.

1986 Topps #161 Jerry Rice rookie. Should retire with every receiving record in the books. Card is up to $50 and will get much higher. Also pick up some '87 and '88 cards as well.

1986 Topps #17 Jay Hilgenberg rookie. A steal at only 75 cents. Buy them up in quantity. No risk.

1986 Topps #119 Karl Mecklenburg rookie. A top quality player for only $2 is a good value. Card is a sleeper, but may not stay that way forever.

1986 Topps #238 Jim Lachey rookie. You can't find a much better player for only $1; again, this card will jump quickly once the public catches on. Buy now, and lots of them.

1987 Topps #310 Ernest Givens rookie. Only $3 and slowly going up every year. I recommend picking them up soon before they double.

1987 Topps #125 Charles Haley rookie. One of the premier defensive stalwarts of the 49'ers, yet no one seems to be touting this card, so here goes. For only $1.25 I'd buy a brick of 100. Should show solid returns down the road.

1987 Topps #362 Jim Kelly. One of the premier quarterbacks in the league. If he can win even one Super Bowl this card will jump dramatically and quickly. Current guide value is $18, but more room to move up.

1988 Topps #66 Pat Swilling rookie. If you want to make money in football cards, take a hard look at defensive players. This guy is one of the best in sacks right now. At 50 cents, another no brainer. Buy up a 100 or 200 at this level.

1989 Topps #45 Thurman Thomas rookie. At $5 this card is a much better value than his '89 Score card which is pushing $50 and one I'd be selling at that high level. No downside on this card. Load up.

1989 Topps #253 Mark Rypien rookie. I like his Topps rookie at $3 a lot more than his Score rookie at $20. Another Super Bowl ring or two and this card will go to the moon. Great value for a proven performer, unlike many other cards selling for much more which are all based on hype and not on the field performance. When buying a card, look at a player's on the field numbers and see if they relate to the asking price of his cards. If most investors did this simple process every time they contemplated a card purchase, you probably would eliminate over 80% of your mistakes you made in the past.

Jack Kemp. The future of his cards lies in his performance in Washington, D.C. Many are gambling he may be vice president or even president some day. I'd pick up one or two if you're a gambler, but only for the long term. Short term should be quiet.

Basketball Cards

The last few years have seen a major interest in the sport of basketball and, as a result, basketball cards as well. What used to be overlooked by most collectors is quite the thing today. Basketball cards are obviously not as popular as baseball cards but their rate of growth has outdone baseball cards easily.

If you like basketball you should definitely pick up some cards for your portfolio. Even if you don't like the game, you should still get some basketball cards. They should prove to be excellent performers down the road.

Here are some cards we feel you should be looking to acquire at this time. Some very good values exist here, so happy hunting.

1948 Bowman #69 George Mikan rookie. The most valuable basketball card in the hobby today. At $3200 in mint, this card has room to move. Prices on this card seem to be jumping up and down. I know of a gem quality piece that sold for $8000 several years ago. Prices are now dropping to a level where it's getting time to buy them up again. Again not for those with small budgets, but if you can afford it I would definitely recommend buying one and forgetting about it for a long time.

1948 Bowman commons. I normally don't recommend commons, but this issue is not common in near mint to mint or mint condition. Commons from the #1-36 series list for $30, #37-72 list for $55 and the scarce play diagram cards list for $30. All are great buys at anywhere near these levels if nm/mt or better. Calling these cards common is one of the biggest misnomers in the hobby there is.

1948 Sports Champions Exhibits George Mikan rookie. You always see the 1948 Bowman Mikan rookie for sale, but when is the last time you saw one of these for sale or at auction? Mint guide value is $450, which is a bargain, if someone will sell it to you for that price. Hunt for this card; you may catch some dealers sleeping on this item. Highly recommended.

1950-51 Scotts Potato Chips George Mikan. Might be the toughest Mikan card of all. Guide value is $2000 in mint, but the bottom line will be finding it and paying what the seller wants, not what the guide lists for a value. Again, this is for the long term hold and one with a large wallet, not for the novice investor.

1952 Bread for Health George Mikan. At $2500 guide value for a mint issue, this lists for only $700 less than his 1948 Bowman rookie card, but this issue is a definite basketball rarity. For one with a large pocketbook and time on his hands, this is the type of investment one should look at. For when the serious investors and collectors start buying, many look for this exact type of item. They like rarity. This easily qualifies and could be selling for multiples of its current value down the road.

1952 Royal Stars George Mikan. Another very scarce regional issue that came off the backs of Royal Desserts boxes. Guide value in mint is $1500, but again a very scarce issue worth buying now for the long run. Make sure it is a nicely cut specimen. That is very important any time you buy any issue like this which is hand cut by collectors, since most were cut by kids who weren't that good with scissors skills at a young age.

1957-58 Topps. As much as this set has gone up in the past three years, this set is still a bargain except for the Bill Russell rookie which is up to $2700 in mint condition. I still like the Russell for the long term especially if mint and centered. This set is notorious for being off-center. I think a mint and centered set could sell for at least a 250% premium over a mint set with normal centering. I'd recommend buying any Hall of Famer. I'd even be buying commons which list for $30 in mint. Again the key is centering on any card you buy from this set. Rumor has it that someone found an entire vending case of this issue last year. Great, now there are thousands of mint and off-center cards added to the market. Seriously though, a good year to buy if you can find what you're looking for.

1960-61 Kahn's Jerry West rookie. One of the most overlooked rookie cards in the basketball field, because most collectors aren't aware of this card. Most dealers push the 1961 Fleer card as his rookie, but this was his first card. It seems the only people who are really aware of the value of this card are the ones who are selling it. Guide value in mint is $600. Vg/ex guide value is $150, yet I've seen dealers asking close to $1000 for one in vg/ex. I haven't seen one in near mint or higher grade in the past decade. This card isn't cheap but once more people become aware of this card and its true scarcity, this card has room to jump to levels of that of Wilt Chamberlain or Bill Russell rookie cards. This card is probably a good buy even in grades as low as very good due to its scarcity. I would obviously try to buy cards in strict near mint or better normally from this era, but if the price is right I would buy lower grade specimen.

1960-61 Kahn's Oscar Robertson rookie. Pretty much the same comments as for the West rookie card. A scarce and rarely seen card. Guide value is $700 in mint, but try and find one at any price. Lots of room to go up especially for a top grade piece.

1961-62 Kahn's Jerry West. Guide value is $300 in mint, but still a good bargain for this scarce regional issue out of the Cincinnati region. Kahn's basketball cards are much scarcer than the baseball issues which aren't that common themselves. This card will continue to go up in value especially if Kahn's cards get more press which they haven't received much in the past.

1961-62 Kahn's Oscar Robertson. Guide value is $300. Basically same comments as on the West card from this year.

1961-62 Bell Brand Jerry West. As tough to find as the '60 Kahn's West card, you will see even less of this card. This west coast regional issue is tough even out here in the Los Angeles area where I reside. Mint guide value is $500 but price isn't the problem. Finding it will be the problem. This card has potential to jump up dramatically the next five years. Commons from this set list at $150, just to give you an idea of how common this issue is.

1961-62 Essex Meats Bob Petit. This regional out of the St. Louis area is a nice little issue that is also seldom seen. Guide value in mint is $125 but try and find them. One of the all-time great forwards and this card is a good buy for the money.

1961-62 Fleers. This issue features the rookie cards of Wilt Chamberlain, Elgin Baylor, Al Attles and Hal Greer. The only cards I see as not great buys right now are the Jerry West and Bill Russell, and that being for the next few years. If you're going to hold for five years or longer then they would be a buy. But as for the rest of the stars in the set, I'd be a buyer. Mint commons are $23 but centering again is a problem. Also all basketball issues from this year or before were not produced in any real quantity and how many were saved in top condition? Probably not many. Be picky and buy nice high grade specimens only. Only buy the set if you can get 100% nm/mt and centered set only. Expect to pay a premium, but it will probably be worth it.

1969-70 Topps. This is Topps' first basketball set since 1958 and different in that the cards were much longer than the normal size cards collectors had become accustomed to. As a result of the big gap in production there are a ton of rookie cards of key players in this particular issue. The key card is the Lew Alcindor rookie. Again, they definitely didn't print many of this issue just like back in 1957. A lot of good cards are in this set. The ones we recommend are:

#1 Wilt Chamberlain. Tough mint card being the first card in the set. Good buy at current guide of $200.

#10 Nate Thurmond. Up to $20 but still a steal! One of the best of his era, a HOF'er and his rookie at this low level. Grab them up.

#15 Connie Hawkins rookie. Just inducted into the HOF. This card is $16 but should be jumping quick and soon.

#20 John Havlicek rookie. $135 and going nowhere right now. I'd be buying one for my portfolio at these levels. No downside, with much upside potential. One of the Celts all-time greats.

#25 Lew Alcindor rookie. His card is down to $850. Used to be double that. Looks like a soft card and the time to buy is when no one else wants it. This card is going back up to its old high and past it the next run up. You can count on it.

#35 Elgin Baylor. Only $60 for this Laker great. I'd put away several at this price level. You should too.

#40 Billy Cunningham rookie. Up to $40 now, but I see a lot more left in this card.

#43 Bill Bradley rookie. Up to $275 and sitting. The price of this card is tied in to his political performance. Buy only for the long run.

#45 Jerry Lucas rookie. Sitting at the $45 range for a while now. A good buy in that price range. Potential to double in value with the next run up in basketball cards.

#50 Oscar Robertson. One of the key non-rookie cards from the set. At $70 not a steal, but one with definite profit potential sitting here down the road.

#55 Dave Bing. A HOF'er, but with the card at only $24 you would wonder. A good value for the buck.

#56 Wes Unseld rookie. At only $33, I'd be buying up a few to put away for a rainy day.

#60 Willis Reed rookie. At $37 but should be much higher.

#80 Earl Monroe rookie. At $42 right now, but seems reasonable at that price.

#84 Hal Greer. A HOF'er for only $8 seems like a bargain to me.

#99 Checklist. A very tough checklist to say the least. Every time I break up a set this is always the first card to sell. Guide value is up to $400 but you don't see much of this card in any grade much less in mint. Of course only buy one that is unmarked.

1970-71 Topps. The second consecutive year for the long oversized cards. This year's production was up from the previous season but still wasn't made in any excess quantities. The key rookie card from this year is the Pete Maravich card.

#1 NBA Scoring Leaders (Alcindor, West, Hayes). The Larry Bird, Julius Erving and Magic Johnson card from 1980-81 is getting a lot of action because it eventually will have three Hall of Famers on one card. Well guess what, this card already has two HOF'ers and Alcindor is on the way. Plus it has a few other things going for it. It's tough to find in high grade being the first card in the set. It's hard to find centered. Plus the price is absurdly cheap in the guides at only $25 in near mint condition. This card is headed for $100+ easily.

#2 NBA Scoring Average (West, Alcindor, Hayes). Another card that's going to have three HOF'ers on one card. Current guide value only $15.

#5 NBA Rebound Leaders (Hayes, Unseld, Alcindor). Another three HOF'ers on one card. Currently at $17. All these leaders cards are a great buy now.

#13 Pat Riley rookie. Going to the HOF as one of the greatest coaches.

#75 Lew Alcindor, 2nd card. Down to $225, starting to look like a great buy.

#90 Nate Thurmond. At $6 an incredible steal!

#100 Oscar Robertson. One of the best, yet this card is still reasonably priced and a buy at its guide value of $43.

#137 Calvin Murphy rookie. A HOF'er as well for only $15 sounds like I'd be buying up some of this player's cards.

#155 Hal Greer. Any 21 year HOF'er card at $5 is worth the gamble, considering there is no real downside involved.

1973-74 Topps #126 Paul Westphal rookie. One of the top guards of his era and slowly rising, but still a bargain at only $8. It was only $3 not too long ago, so obviously someone out there is buying the card to make it go up.

1974-75 Topps #196 George Gervin rookie. One of the premier guards of his era and the card is finally starting to move up the past year. It's at $22 right now, but a lot more movement left in this card.

1975-76 Topps #254 Moses Malone rookie. A future Hall of Famer for sure, but I don't see too many investors snapping up this card, at least not yet. It's up to $88 and just keeps going up year after year. Should start taking off when he nears induction down the road, but the time to buy is now.

1977-78 Topps #111 Robert Parish rookie. This card was dead for years until many finally figured out that this Celtic is also headed for the HOF after retirement. It's up to $35 but it should continue to go up for many more years as he nears induction into immortality in Springfield.

1979-80 Topps #31 Alex English rookie. One of the top forwards of the 1980s. The card finally started moving in the past year and is up to $22 but not done running up.

1980-81 Topps #34-174-139 Larry Bird (rookie) Julius Erving, Magic Johnson (rookie). One of the most desirable rookie cards of the 1980's with one Hall of Famer on the card and two more on the way. Current guide value is up to $400, but I have seen widespread prices on this card. Make sure to buy them without the distracting black printing marks on the front of the card and get one that is nicely centered. Also get this card in nm/mt or better grade. Pay a little extra but get top quality. This is always true, but on certain cards like this it is doubly important. Especially when you go to sell.

1981-82 Topps #4 Larry Bird. The second card and first single card of this future HOF'er. This card is at $30 right now, but has lots of interest since his rookie card is too expensive for some collectors and investors.

1981-82 Topps #21 Magic Johnson. A lot of collectors aren't that fond of group shot rookie cards like Magic's first card, so they chase after his first solo card such as this one. This one is up to $40 in near mint, but has a lot of room to go up since his rookie card sells for about ten times as much right now. A solid buy at current levels.

1981-82 Topps #E75 Kevin McHale rookie. Another Celtic from this rookie class who will be joining Larry Bird in Springfield after he retires. Currently $20, but guaranteed not to stay this reasonable forever.

In **1983** the **Star Co.** started producing basketball cards. The one thing they had going for them was limited production—not limited to what we see today from most card companies but truly limited issues. I don't think they ever produced more than 10,000 of any one issue. Some were limited to less than 1000. This is why their cards bring big prices. They are scarce. I'm sure that not being that popular when they were released, many got either thrown away or destroyed in one way or another. These cards probably represent some of the best cards from the 1980s. Too bad more collectors aren't aware of these cards or their scarcity. If these cards do catch on, the prices could go much higher than they are currently.

The 1986 Fleer set lists over 50 rookies cards in their set, but most are actually rookies from the various Star Co. sets issued previous to the 1986 Fleer cards.

The problem lies in our hobby not having any standards of what a rookie is. Whatever you want to be a rookie can be a rookie if that's what you want it to be. This controversy will never end and comments such as these will not bring it any closer to being settled.

Here is one of the best Star Co. cards to buy currently:

1984-85 Star Co. #101 Michael Jordan rookie. Only 4000 team sets were made so there can only be a maximum of 4000 Jordan rookies out there. Obviously some have been lost or damaged. I doubt if there are more than 1500 of this card left in mint condition. Current guide value is $800 in mint but that will slowly but surely go up in value for one of the most exciting players ever to touch a basketball in any era.

1986-87 Fleer Wax Case. If you have $50,000+ laying around and don't know what to do with it you may want to buy a case of this scarce commodity. When they hit $20,000 I thought that would be close to the top for this item. Obviously that hasn't been the case. Today there can't be more than 100 sealed cases of this product. As the price gets higher more and more get broken up to be sold by the box or the pack. Some day a true factory sealed case may be as rare as a 1952 Topps case.

If you can't afford a case, you may wish to acquire a wax box which contains 36 packs. They currently sell for $4000+. If you can't afford a box, buy a pack or two. Current value is around $125.

1986-87 Fleer. The premier set of this firm's cards is popular to say the least and not for one on a small budget. The set is up to $800 already and slowly rising month after month. I'd concentrate on some key players such as:

#7 Charles Barkley
#26 Clyde Drexler
#27 Joe Dumars
#57 Michael Jordan
#68 Karl Malone
#77 Chris Mullin
#109 Isaiah Thomas
#121 Dominique Wilkins
#131 James Worthy

Most guides list most of the above cards as rookies when their first cards were issued by the Star Co. in previous years. I would buy some of each to play it safe.

Hockey Cards

Of the four major sportcard categories, hockey has to be the least collected or invested in today. I see that trend changing slowly but surely. Interest in hockey in the United States today is the strongest it ever has been and getting stronger. More collectors in the U.S. are now starting to collect hockey cards. Plus the smart investors are jumping into this, the market with the most potential in the card market today.

With a new league president coming in, let's hope his leadership will help get a major television contract for the U.S. and help hockey get much more public attention than it's getting right now.

We will concentrate mostly on Parkhurst cards that were produced from 1951 to 1964, O-Pee-Chee cards from 1968 to 1988 and Topps cards from 1954 to 1988.

PARKHURST

1951-52. These were the first cards produced in the modern era of hockey. These cards are scarce but doubly so in near mint or higher grades. I recommend the purchase of any Hall of Famer right now as their prices seem too cheap. One guide has commons in nm at $25, yet Hall of Famers are only $10 more. That is absurd. I'd be buying these cards more for the long term hold where the profits will be maximized. Go after the key cards now such as Gordie Howe, Maurice Richard, Terry Sawchuck, Doug Harvey, Red Kelly and Ted Lindsay. All '51 Parkies as they are also called are worth more than guide. Buy any cards from this series if you can find them in near mint or better condition.

1952-53. Similar to the '51 Parkies, this issue is also scarce in high grade. Again the HOF'er cards are downright cheap in most cases. These cards list for less than the '51 Parkies, yet some feel these cards are tougher in high grades. I agree and feel they should be selling for as much as the '51's if not a bit more. Time will tell on this theory. Load up on HOF'ers, especially #1 Richard. Also recommended for the long term hold.

1953-54. I love '50's Parkies cards. They are attractive and scarce cards. Yet the prices are not of out sight, at least not yet. The key rookies this year are #27 Jean Beliveau, #53 Gump Worsley and #56 Andy Bathgate. I'd be loading up on all the HOF'ers again and any rookie card of a star player. You probably won't find that much to buy, but be selective and buy anything nice. Be careful as centering can be awful on Parkie cards.

1954-55. Only one key rookie came out of this set, that being Johnny Bower #65. Again I like any HOF'er card from this set as most are too cheap for cards almost 40 years old. I'd especially be on the look for cards #97-99. They were action shots and these three cards featured the first card of HOF'er Jacques Plante. Most guides list his '55 Parkie card as his rookie, but here is his first appearance. At $60 each they are a bargain considering his 1955 card is at $350 in nm.

1955-56. Due to its price, many overlook the scarcity of this issue which some experts feel is the scarcest Parkhurst issue. It is definitely the biggest sleeper of the Parkie issues that we are discussing here. NM/MT or mint cards are virtually impossible to find. The key rookie is the #50 Jacques Plante. The set contains 40 HOF'ers, many of whom are All-Time greats. As I write this there are only four cards which list for over $100 in near mint condition. We are talking bargain time here. But the problem will be finding high grade specimens, and they WILL cost you over guide, unless you find a dealer sleeping on the job.

In the past few years I have bought complete runs of Parkie sets, yet they all didn't have this set in the run. Does that tell you something?

Our highest recommendation on this year's cards. Even commons at $12 are a big time bargain.

1957-58. This set features only cards of Toronto and Montreal players. Yet nine of the Canadians from this team became HOF'ers. Henri Richard and Frank Mahovlich were the key rookies this year. I would concentrate on acquiring any HOF'er from this set. They are low as $20 in the guide for some. Hard to believe, isn't it?

1958-59. Another set with just Toronto and Montreal players only. But we have 19 HOF'ers in this set which represents 38 percent of the entire set in just superstars. No key rookies, but headed up by players like Richard, Beliveau and Plante. Go after the Hall of Famers as they again are priced way too reasonable in my opinion.

1959-60. No key rookies this year, but again filled with a lot of HOF'ers. This was again a Toronto-and-Montreal-only issue. Nothing spectacular; the printing was definitely down from the previous few years, but again the price doesn't yet reflect this fact. Pick up any high grade HOF'ers at current levels which are reasonable to say the least.

1960-61. This year Detroit was added to the Toronto and Montreal only issues of the past few years. No key rookies are in this set, but this was the last card of Maurice Richard and one last time for Gordie Howe and Maurice Richard to appear in the same card set. Except for Howe, again all the Hall of Famers are priced right for you the investor to buy them up.

1961-62. Only key rookie this year is #5 Dave Keon, but there are 18 HOF'er cards in this issue which are very difficult in grades above near mint. I also believe they cut back on production again this year, as I've heard from many dealers who specialize in hockey cards. Again, except for the Howe card, the Hall of Famers are a great buy at this time.

1962-63. The is the most common Parkie set ever produced. There are no key rookie cards in the set, but there are 21 HOF'ers in this issue which means almost 40 percent of the set is HOF'ers. There are two Gordie Howe cards in this set, but again, the rest of the stars are cheap. For example, commons list for $9 in near mint and #5 Red Kelly, a HOF'er, is just $10. A HOF'er at just a 10 percent premium over a common. Try and buy a baseball card with those numbers in mind and I doubt if you'll even come close to buying one card.

Even though this is the easiest Parkhurst hockey set of all, there are two cards, technically part of the set, which are not common; as a matter of fact, they are very scarce. There is an unnumbered checklist card which lists for $165 in near mint. There is also a tally or contest card which most guides don't even acknowledge, probably because they don't know of its existence. I know of the checklist card trading upwards of $400 in mint and unchecked condition. The contest card sells for $200-300 depending on the grade. Both are on most collectors' want lists, but seldom seen for sale in any grade.

Hockey cards are an area fertile with superb buys. Don't fall into the trap of saying "I don't know who Plante and Beliveau are," or "I don't like hockey." We are trying to show you how to buy cards which can make you money, BIG money in many cases. Don't let your ignorance of the sport stop your investment goals.

1963-64. The last Parkie set is also one of the best efforts visually. The Gordie Howe card with the American flag in the background is absolutely a classic card if I ever saw one. The only key rookie is that of Jacques Laperriere. This set has 31 HOF'ers and except for Gordie Howe, the most expensive is $56. Again I strongly encourage you to pick up ANY Hall of Famer. I can't see how you can go wrong with any of these cards in the long run. These represent far greater value than buying a new untried rookie for $10 or more. That is speculation, buying Parkhurst cards is investing.

TOPPS

1954-55. This very popular set is historic in that it is the first American hockey set. For years many thought the Gordie Howe card from this set was his rookie card. Then we south of the Canadian border realized there was such a thing as Parkhurst cards which preceded Topps hockey cards. The cards in this set are very attractive and are considered condition rarities. You will have great difficulty finding cards in near mint or better grades. What are the best cards to buy from this year? Well, about the only cards which are not grossly undervalued are the Gordie Howe and Terry Sawchuck cards. The rest of the stars are excellent buys. I would even recommend commons from this set which guide at $25 in near mint. A highly recommended year for hockey cards.

1957-58. After a two-year hiatus Topps came back with this issue. The key rookie cards this year are Johnny Bucyk, Glenn Hal, Pierre Pilote and Norm Ullman. The Howe and Sawchuck cards are again the key star cards from this set. I would concentrate on the Hall of Famers from this set which are not overpriced at current levels. Also try and find cards that are nice and glossy. For some reason many are found without this, though they are supposed to come with it. Be careful that they haven't been reglossed though.

1958-59. Two thirds of the entire value of this set is card #66, the father of current super-star Brett Hull. Many call it the Bobby Hull set because this card IS the set. The card is his rookie, the last card in the set and one of the key rookies of the 1950s or of any decade for that matter. Guide value is $2200 in near mint, but this card is selling for $3000-4000 in higher grades, when it surfaces, which is not that often. Only two other cards in the set list for $100 or more, those being the cards of Howe and Sawchuck. Commons list for $10, yet some HOF'ers list for $12. More bargains exist. Can you believe all these deals? Buy all you can in nm or better grades. Even the Hull is a great buy, but stick with nm/mt or mint only. You will have to pay dearly for the privilege, but it's always fun to sell killer cards like this down the road for record prices.

1959 - 60. Topps last set of the decade didn't have any important rookie cards. Key cards are Bobby Hull's second card and Gordie Howe. Get used to seeing Mr. Howe's name for a long time, how did you think he tallied so many records? He was a great player and kept producing year after year. I would be going after HOF'ers cards in this year as they list for as low as $12 in near mint.

A couple of points to remember when searching for these cards. The cards may have gone up in value by the time you are looking for them. Many dealers may not agree with the values assigned by the price guides. So a card may list for $12, but they may want $15 or even $20 for the card. If a card is in nm/mt or mint, you will obviously pay way over guide to buy the card. If a card is hot when you're looking to purchase, this could add an additional premium to the card. If you're looking for Gordie Howe cards in Detroit add an additional premium for that privilege. Do you buy Gem Mint type quality? Guess what, add a premium for this again. Obviously a $12 card can go for double or triple guide with absolutely no problem. The key is for you to ascertain if the asking price is within reason for the card in the current market in which you are buying.

One way is to find out the dealer's buy price for the card he is selling. The closer to his retail that he is paying, the more accurate his asking price is. For example, if a dealer is willing to pay 70 percent to 80 percent of his asking price, that's being fair. But if the dealer is only willing to pay 50 percent or less or worse yet won't even quote you a buy price, maybe the dealer ripped the card for 50 percent of guide value and is now marking the card up 300-400 percent. This is a common practice, I can assure you.

Also if he won't buy it, try and give it to him to sell it for you on a consignment basis. That way you should be able to get a pretty strong wholesale price for a card that he is selling for a big price. If this fails, you will have to ask why is he selling the card for way over guide but isn't interested in YOUR card at anywhere near that level.

I use this approach and just ask why he can quote such big numbers on the sell side of the equation, but on the buying end there is such a disparity. ASK him to explain himself to you. I think you have a right to know why a dealer is asking a certain price. If he doesn't give you the courtesy of an answer, maybe you should find a new dealer. Don't worry, there are a lot of dealers in the business today, so you can find several new ones to deal with.

1960-61. The first set of the decade featured some of the all-time greats of days passed. This set of 66 cards contains almost 40 Hall of Famers. The only key rookie was a good one, Stan Mikita, the Chicago Blackhawks star. The key cards from this set represent a good buy at this time. The All-Time greats are a solid value at current guide values. Some of these cards are single prints, such as cards #47, #59 and #60.

1961-62. One of the most common sets of the era features the rookie cards of Jean Ratelle and Rod Gilbert. Bobby Hull and Stan Mikita's second card are the key stars of the set. Again we see HOF'ers from this set at small premiums over common cards. This would tell us the stars are a good buy currently. Also card #66 is a checklist card. This card lists for $175 in nm condition. A baseball checklist card from 1961 lists for less than $10. This may give you some idea of how few hockey cards were produced compared to baseball of the same era. It may also give you an idea of how few unmarked high grade hockey checklist cards still remain today. Hockey experts feel hockey checklist cards are even scarcer than their price indicates. I like checklist cards and would buy them especially if nm/mt and unmarked of course. Never buy marked checklist cards no matter how cheap.

1962-63. Another set which was produced in quantity. The problem today is they are not available in high grade in quantity. The blue bordered cards chip so easily that they show immediate wear, similar to 1971 baseball cards.

The set lacks any key rookie cards. Bobby Hull and Stan Mikita are the key star cards from this set. Again we see the HOF'ers from this set at very reasonable levels and would recommend them. Card #66 is the checklist card, at $85 sounds like an excellent value if you can locate a sharp specimen.

1963-64. This was the last year Topps had competition from Parkhurst as they bailed out of the hockey card market after this season. Actually it left Topps without any competition until just a couple of years ago. Judging from their product over this time frame, it just goes to show you what you get when there is no competition. Compare that to today's cards. Competition is fierce and see the quality cards we have gotten. A poor product gets killed almost immediately and you can't give it away, literally.

Key card from this set is the Bobby Hull card. Again card #66 is the checklist card—buy it. I'm still recommending buying up the HOF'ers from this year as well. Will good deals never cease?

1964-65. This was Topps' first set without competition. They went to the oversized card, printed it in two series, with the second series #56-#110 being tough for collectors putting sets together. There were several single printed cards; they are: #58, #59, #72, #73, #74, #80, #91, #92, #99, #105, and #106.

This set marked the return of Gordie Howe to a Topps set, as well as the first Topps cards of such players such as Henri Richard, Frank Mahovlich, Jean Beliveau and Dave Keon.

Gordie Howe and Bobby Hull are the only key cards in this set which weren't single prints.

We recommend acquiring the checklist cards #54 and #55. We think the second series cards are still an excellent value, if you can find them in nm/mt condition which won't be an easy task, especially the single print cards.

Again, chase after any HOF'er card. Many are priced for those on a budget.

Card #92, Marcel Paille, rookie card, is one of the toughest cards in the set. It's one of the single prints and lists for $375. I've seen this card for sale at levels approaching the four figure mark. Seems to be the key card of the set. Only buy this card if nm or better and don't pay an obscene premium for it.

1965-66. This set is headed up by the rookie cards of Phil Esposito, Ed Giacomin, Gerry Cheevers and Yvan Cournoyer. The key star cards are those of Bobby Hull and two cards of Gordie Howe. One of those cards, #122, is a tribute to Howe's 600th goal in the NHL. It is one of seven cards which were single printed; the single prints were cards #122-#128, the last seven cards in the set. This particular Howe card is very popular and lists for $350 in nm, but dealers usually are getting over this when they have them for sale. The rest of the single print cards are all team cards and are popular with collectors trying to complete this set, especially the last card, #128, the Boston Bruins card.

There are two checklist cards, #66 and #121. Both should be bought if they can be bought in top grades.

Go after the HOF'ers from this set as they are all quiet right now, which is the best time to buy anything, rather than when they are red hot.

The Esposito rookie is also a good value at its current guide value of $390 as is the #122 Gordie Howe 600 goals card we mentioned earlier.

1966-67. I guess we can call this the "Bobby Orr" set. This one card is almost 2/3 of the complete set's value. It's at $1900 in nm, but high grade specimens this past year have sold for prices starting at $2700 in mint up to one piece which supposedly fetched $7,000.

There are no other key rookie cards worth mentioning and the key star cards are Howe, Hull and Esposito, who have seven cards between them.

This set is similar to the 1955 Bowman baseball issue, the T.V. type with the wood grain border. Thus we now have a condition rarity. The cards are not hard to find, but in nm/mt or mint they can be downright nasty to locate, and centering may pose another problem.

There are two checklists, #66 and #120. Both are tough in choice condition. That's why you want to get them.

I suggest getting any star card or HOF'er especially if nm/mt or mint. These cards represent good value at current guide values. This is one set where you will have to pay over guide even in near mint to buy them.

These cards are undervalued in nm/mt or mint condition. But if they will stay so forever is the question. I doubt it.

1967-68. A very attractive set of cards which is the last issue with the six original NHL teams before Topps merged with O-Pee-Chee the next year.

The key rookie cards from this set are Rogie Vachon,

Jacques Lemaire and Derek Sanderson. The key star cards are Bobby Orr's second cards, three of them, as well as Gordie Howe and Phil Esposito.

The two checklist cards are #66 and #120. Both are on our buy list.

The HOF'ers and their star cards in this set I feel are selling for less than they should. I recommend all the key cards from this set as well.

1968-69. This was the first year of both Topps and OPC (O-Pee-Chee) cards. OPC sets would normally be much larger than the Topps issues from each year. Thus the OPC sets usually sell for a lot more than its Topps counterpart. Also many times the OPC cards seem to be harder to find, especially here in the U.S. Another problem with OPC cards is their quality control. The cards seem to be plagued with poor centering. Many come with a rough cut as a normal thing. Thus if you find cards without the rough cut edges, that's scarce and worth a premium. Also the paper stock on some years seemed to be inferior and that didn't help to find high quality OPC cards.

The key rookie card from this set is the Bernie Parent card. The key star cards are those of Bobby Orr and Gordie Howe.

The checklist card is #121; buy this card. The last cards of Pierre Pilote and Marcel Pronovost at $8 and $5 are a good buy.

Also go after the cheap HOF'er cards from this set, of which there are almost 20 in the under $20 price range in nm.

1969-70. Not one of the most exciting offerings from Topps, but it does contain the rookie card of Serge Savard. The key star cards are Bobby Hull, Gordie Howe and Bobby Orr. The cards to be chasing would be all the HOF'er cards under $25 and the #132 checklist card.

1970-71. The first set of this decade was a very large production run. The key rookie cards are those of Brad Park and Gilbert Perreault. The key star cards are Bobby Orr and Gordie Howe. The best buys from this set are #1 Cheevers, #3 Orr, #11 Esposito, #40 Worsley, #78 Parent, #132 Checklist.

1971-72. A nice, clean looking set, but off-center cards seems to plague this series. The Ken Dryden rookie is the only major first year card from this set. The key star cards are Gordie Howe, Bobby Hull and Bobby Orr.

The best buys would be #40 Park, #45 Dryden, #60 Perreault, #70 Howe, #111 Checklist, #114 Clarke, #125 Mikita.

Looking at some of the other HOF'ers in the set they still seem too cheap, and look like they represent a good buy for their inexpensive prices currently. Many of the HOF'ers are only $3.50 in nm at guide prices. Again, you can buy real value or pay many times this for new card hype. Reality always sets into all hot and hyped markets, be it real estate or classic cars. Then, as we have seen in those two markets, they come crashing down to reality and fast. Don't you be a victim of new card hype.

The past few months I've noticed a trend of new investors wanting to sell out of their modern late 1980s cards and, even worse, the 1990's cards and wanting to invest in blue chip type material. Too bad they couldn't have figured this out before they made their initial investment.

1972-73. Topps stepped up production again with this year's set. But the quality control didn't seem to be the greatest. Off-center cards, diagonally cut cards, miscut cards on the backs, print problems seem to plague this series. The cards may not be numerically scarce, but as usual, they aren't common in top grades. No older cards are.

The key cards in this set are the first Topps cards of Guy Lafleur and HOF'er Marcel Dionne, also Dryden's second card.

The best buys in this set are #18 Dionne, #79 Lafleur, #160 Dryden. I keep looking at the HOF prices in the set and see many of them in the under $10 range. I guess we should try and pick up some at these low levels.

1973-74. The rookie cards of Billy Smith and Bill Barber head up this colorful set.

Besides the key rookies, the HOF'ers at under $5 each seem like a bargain. Almost 20 years old, a Hall of Famer for under $5. Doesn't anybody care about a proven player or have we just forgotten about retired players? If you think like me, put your money where you get real value, minimal downside and cards with liquidity when you're ready to sell.

1974-75. This year's set was expanded to 264 cards with rookies like Lanny McDonald and Denis Potvin heading up the set. Bobby Orr is the key star card in this set.

The cards I would concentrate on would again be the HOF'ers. Most can be had for less than $5 each. Sounds like a deal of the week.

1975-76. At 330 cards this was the largest Topps hockey set. But it lacks any major rookie cards. The three checklist cards #99, #171, #267 are only $6 and an excellent value for the money.

This was another year where Topps pumped up production as these cards are definitely not hard to come by.

1976-77. A pretty mediocre set to say the least. It has the Bryan Trottier rookie and a Bobby Orr card. Not much else to say about the set except for these two cards.

1977-78. The only things here worth mentioning are the Bryan Trottier second card, Rod Gilbert and Ed Giacomin's last cards for this set that again saw heavy production.

1978-79. A real dog set. Only rookies of note are the Mike Bossy and Doug Wilson first cards. Also has the last cards of HOF'ers Yvan Cournoyer, Jacques Lemaire and Bernie Parent. Topps again made a heavy production run this year, but on top of that the cards were poorly cut as well as a notorious bad year for centering. Mediocre set at best.

1979-80. Again we have one card that dominates this set. Card #18 is 2/3 of the entire set's value. That of course is the "Great One", Wayne Gretzy. I really think that title belongs to Gordie Howe, but that's open to discussion. Right now this card is sitting still. Only buy this card for the long term.

A few other cards worth chasing are the last cards of #85 Cheevers, #150 Dryden, #155 Mikita, #175 Howe, #185 Hull.

1980-81. A tough set for collectors not familiar with hockey since the names of the players are only found on the front of the card under a scratch-off material. Without a keen knowledge of players' faces you will have to look up each card in a guide to figure out which player you have, which of course would mostly apply to commons, not the bigger names. This was an interesting concept, but since they haven't repeated it, I assume the experiment bombed.

The key card in this set is the second card of Wayne Gretzky. The key rookie cards are those of Michel Goulet, Ray Bourque, Mike Gartner. Also, here we have the last card of Phil Esposito.

Best bets are the Goulet, Gartner and Gretzky cards.

1981-82. Topps decided to issue this year's cards in regions, West and East. This was also Topps' last hockey set for two years.

The key cards from this set are the rookie cards of Jari Kurri, Peter Stastny, and Denis Savard.

The best bets are the three previously mentioned rookie cards and the third card of Wayne Gretzky. This card is not very tough to find but is an excellent value for the money as any earlier cards of Gretzky are much more expensive.

1984-85. After a two year break from producing hockey cards, Topps came back with this year's set. The key cards are the rookie cards of Steve Yzerman and Pat LaFontaine and also the first Topps card of Paul Coffey. Two-thirds of this year's cards were double printed and the other one third were single prints.

Best Bets: Yzerman, LaFontaine, Coffey.

1985-86. A very average set, but this includes the premier player in the NHL today, the Pittsburgh Penguins' Mario Lemieux. This card is worth over half of the entire set's value by itself. Other key cards from this set are the rookie cards of Pelle Lindbergh and Tomas Sandstrom as well as Steve Yzerman's second card.

With a second straight Stanley Cup victory for Pittsburgh, cards of all Penguins cards are in demand with Mario Lemieux's cards leading the way. His rookie cards have jumped 33 percent since the Stanley Cup Victory recently.

Best Bets: Lemieux, Yzerman, Dionne, Larmer, Goulet, Kurri.

1986-87. Topps continued with another very unexciting hockey set. The key cards from this set are the rookie card of superstar goalie Patrick Roy, the second card of Mario Lemieux, the first Topps card of Al MacInnis, Wayne Gretzky and Steve Yzerman.

Best bets: Roy, Lemieux, Messier, MacInnis, Yzerman.

1987-88. The key cards to this set are the rookie cards of Luc

Robitaille, Adam Oates, Jimmy Carson, Esa Tikkanen and Rick Tocchet. Other noteworthy cards are those of Wayne Gretzky and Patrick Roy.

Best bets: Lemieux, Robitaille, Roy, Messier, Yzerman, Hatcher.

1988-89. This set made the name Hull famous a second time, this time with the son of Bobby Hull, Brett Hull. His rookie card was one of the hottest cards on the market soon after it came out. Now it's topped out price wise and is sitting quietly waiting for Brett to do some more record shattering feats.

Other key cards from this set are the rookie cards of Joe Nieuwendyk, Brendan Shanahan and Pierre Turgeron. Also a very popular card is the card #120 of Wayne Gretzky in his "sweater" pose. The Hull rookie and Gretzky sweater card are two-thirds of the entire sets value alone.

Best bets: Hull (long term), Nieuwendyk.

O-PEE-CHEE

After not producing hockey cards for almost three decades, O-Pee-Chee, more commonly referred to in print as OPC, made a return to the hockey card wars in 1968.

Trying to find their cards centered or without a rough cut problem can pose a serious problem to the collector or investor looking for top grade specimens of these cards. Also they are much scarcer south of the Canadian border and tend to be more popular with collectors than their Topps counterparts and thus usually are more expensive than a same year Topps issue.

1968-69. One of the more popular OPC issues since it was the first one since the 1930s. The key rookie card is that of Bernie Parent. Other key cards are those of Bobby Orr, Bobby Hull, Gordie Howe and Terry Sawchuck.

Best bets: Orr (all), Hull, Esposito, Worsle, Parent, Bower, Horton, Plante, Mikita, Checklist cards #61 and #121.

1969-70. The key rookies from this year's set are those of Serge Savard and Tony Esposito. Other key cards are those of Bobby Orr, Gordie Howe and Bobby Hull.

Best bets: Worsley, Beliveau, Orr, Esposito, Howe, Plante, Sawchuck, Howe #193, #31 and #132 Checklist cards.

1970-71. The key rookie cards from this set are the cards of Brad Park, Gilbert Perreault, Bobby Clarke and Darryl Sittler, Guy Lapointe.

Best bets: Orr, Howe, Savard, Park, Parent, T. Esposito, G. Lapointe, and #231 Sawchuck.

1971-72. The key rookies in this year's set are Ken Dryden, Marcel Dionne who just got voted in to hockey's Hall of Fame and Guy LaFleur.

Best bets: P. Esposito, Perreault, Orr, Clarke, Dionne, LaFleur, Sittler, #262 Howe.

1972-73. This set lacks any major rookies, and the key cards are those of Bobby Hull, Gordie Howe and Ken Dryden.

Best bets: Dionne, Clarke, LaFleur, Orr, Dryden, Mikita, Sittler, Hull.

1973-74. The key rookie cards are those of Larry Robinson, Billy Smith and Bill Barber.

Best bets: Mikita, Dionne, Orr, Clarke, LaFleur, T. Esposito, Sittler, B Smith, Robinson.

1974-75. The key rookies from this set are Don Cherry, Lanny McDonald, Dennis Potvin, Glenn Resch and Bob Gainey.

Best bets: Dionne, Orr, Dryden, McDonald, Potvin, LaFleur, Robinson, Gainey.

1975-76. No major rookies appear in this set.

Best bets: Orr, Dionne, Robinson, Clarke, Gainey, McDonald, Smith.

1976-77. The only major rookie card in this year's set is that of Bryan Trottier.

Best bets: Parent, Gainey, Dionne, Trottier, Robinson, LaFleur, Potvin, Dryden, Orr, P. Esposito, McDonald.

1977-78. No major rookie cards are found in this year's set.

Best bets: Robinson, Dryden, McDonald, Gainey, Mikita, Lafleur, B. Smith, Dionne, Orr.

1978-79. The key rookie cards out of this set are Mike Bossy, Doug Wilson and Dave Taylor.

Best bets: Trottier, Dryden, Mikita, Gainey, LaFleur, Bossy, Dionne, Robinson, D. Taylor.

1979-80. This set has only one valuable rookie card in it, but what a rookie card. Wayne Gretzky, the player who has rewritten the record books. This card represents about 70 percent of the entire set's value. At its current value it's not a steal, but represents more of a long term hold.

Best bets: Gretzky, Howe, Hull, Dionne, Bossy, LaFleur.

1980-81. The key rookies this year are Brian Propp, Michel Goulet, Ray Bourque, Mike Gartner, Mark Messier, Rod Langway.

Best bets: Dionne, Goulet, Esposito, Bourque, Gartner, Robinson, Gretzky, Messier.

1981-82. The key rookies from this year's set are Denis Savard, Jari Kurri, Andy Moog and Peter Stastny.

Best bets: Gartner, Goulet, LaFleur, Dionne, Robinson, Messier, Gretzky, McDonald.

1982-83. The key rookies are Grant Fuhr, Ron Francis, Joe Mullen and Dale Hawerchuk.

Best bets: Bourque, Coffey, Messier, Dionne, Goulet, Gartner.

1983-84. The key rookie cards this year are Phil Housley, Steve Larmer, Bernie Nichols, Brian Bellows, Pelle Lindbergh.

Best bets: Coffey, Fuhr, Gretzky, Messier, Bourque, Dionne, LaFleur, Gartner.

1984-85. The top rookies this year are Steve Yzerman, Pat La-Fontaine, Chris Chelios and Cam Neely.

Best bets: Bourque, Larmer, Yzerman, Gartner, Coffey, Kurri, Neely.

1985-86. The key rookies are Al MacInnis, Tomas Sandstrom and the key card of the 1980s, the Mario Lemieux rookie. The Lemieux card is almost half of the entire set's value, and for good reason. He is the best in the league today.

Best bets: Lemieux, Coffey, Goulet.

1986-87. The key rookie card in this set is Patrick Roy.

Best bets: Yzerman, Roy, Lemieux, Messier.

1987-88. The key rookie cards this year are Rick Tocchet, Esa Tikanen, Bill Ranford, Luc Robitaille, Jimmy Carson, Adam Oates and Stephane Richer.

Best bets: Lemieux, Robitaille, Messier, Oates, Roy.

1988-89. The key card in this set is the Brett Hull rookie. This card is worth 60 percent of the entire set. It is worth around $100 now and I don't expect much to happen short term, but long term this card should do fine.

A lot of investors seem to shy away from any sport they don't like or follow. I feel you should definitely try to change your thinking to make sure you diversify enough to take advantage of any market which could really take off, like this one. Even if you only put 10 percent of your money into hockey, you should own some hockey cards. You won't be sorry.

Money-Saving Questions and Answers

Q: If I wanted to invest in just one area of baseball cards, what would be the best place? I'm a conservative investor, have $5,000 to spend a year and can hold the cards for 5 years or longer. What do you recommend I buy?

A: I think you can't go wrong buying Topps and Bowman cards from 1948-1959. A lot of classic cards came from this area. The cards here are scarce in high grades, there is a lot of demand here, always has been and always will be. Cards here are usually very saleable be they rookies, stars or even commons. This is classic blue chip type material. For your budget, hold period and goals, I think you can't go too far wrong in this segment of the baseball card market.

Q: I see cards advertised as Gem Mint. What is a Gem Mint card and what is its value as compared to a mint grade card?

A: Basically a Gem Mint card means the card is in mint condition, but may have exceptional gloss, color, perfect centering or other features which may not be normal for the card in question. For example, 1953

Topps cards don't come perfect. If you can find a specimen without a rough cut, full gloss, without chipping on the bottom border etc., this card could qualify as a Gem Mint card.

Determining the value is a little harder to do since NO price guides have ever tackled this matter. It's just a matter of how much over the mint value a Gem Mint card should bring. Obviously a 1953 Topps card in Gem Mint is worth a larger premium than a 1974 Topps card in the same grade. There is no set premium for Gem Mint over Mint. Every issue is different. So some issues may command only a 20 percent premium yet an issue like a T-205 Gold Border tobacco issue in Gem condition could bring a premium of 500 percent or more over the same card in mint condition. The price spread between Mint and Gem Mint will get wider and wider for older issues in the years to come.

Q: I keep hearing that the Japanese are getting into the American card market. Is that true? What effect will that have on the card market?

A: So far the Japanese haven't gotten into our market big time. If they do, you will know it. They will probably buy everything that isn't tied down. It won't take too many millions of dollars to make our market rock 'n' roll. One or two big investment syndicates could cause the market to jump dramatically in a short period of time, but so far we haven't seen it. I think you will know it if it happens. There is no way for a lot of money to enter our market without everyone hearing about it.

Q: Does a card have to be centered to be graded Mint condition?

A: I say no, but others say a card has to be centered to be mint. Since our hobby has NO grading standard, which is hard to believe, it's a matter of who you deal with. I feel a card can be off-center and yet be mint. Of course a card that is off-center will not be worth as much as a card which is mint and centered. I feel less than 5 percent of older cards are centered. Newer cards tend to be much better centered due to the far superior quality control. Thus if you're looking for older cards that are perfectly centered, you are NOT going to be buying many mint cards if this is the standard you are going to use.

For example, 1959 Bob Gibson cards don't come centered 50/50. A 70/30 centered example is more the norm. Also what about the reverse? For example 1976 Dennis Eckersley rookie cards are hard to find centered. Yet if you find one centered on the FRONT, you will find it off-center on the reverse. So if you're looking for this card centered front and back, I think that may be in the RARE category. Centering today is very important with collectors and investors alike. Yet if you get too picky on centering, again, you won't be buying many cards issued before 1989.

Learn what the normal centering is for certain cards. Some cards just may not be around in 50/50 centering or even 55/45. It's pretty futile looking for something that may not even exist.

Q: Which promo cards do you feel have the best investment potential?

A: Any you can get for free. That way you have zero downside risk. Remember virtually all promo cards are given away. Then you see prices rise, some little, some to over $1000 each. As soon as they rise they magically come down in price and usually then you can't find many buyers. Leave promo cards to collectors and the speculators. They are usually a poor investment unless, as I stated earlier, you can get them for free.

Q: Are counterfeit cards a problem for today's investor and what should one be on the lookout for?

A: Counterfeit cards were never much of a problem in the hobby until prices started rising dramatically. Then we started seeing this problem arise somewhat. Fortunately, virtually all were easily detectable and no real problem existed. Then the counterfeiters turned their attention to any new hot rookie card. If any new card ever started receiving heavy collector/investor demand, there was a good chance someone would try to make copies of it. Again, most seemed to be detectable.

Sadly not very much had been done to educate the public to this problem. But recently NASDAM, a national dealers association, and Bob Lemke, the editor of *Sports Collectors Digest*, just published a book that give purchasers of cards a way to help detect counterfeit cards. They have published a book called *Sportcard Counterfeit Detector*. The first issue lists 93 known counterfeit cards and how to detect phony issues.

The key to not being a victim of counterfeit cards is to know what the card issue is supposed to look like. Know your dealer.

This is probably your best defense. Counterfeit cards tend to be sold cheaper than the real thing so they can sell as many as possible since their cost factor is obviously very little in most cases and the selling price is almost pure profit. So beware if the price sounds too good. Last year two dealers in the San Francisco area got burned for $75,000 purchasing counterfeit Jose Canseco rookie cards. The price they paid was a tipoff that something was wrong. The amount of cards involved should have been the second tipoff. The quality of the cards should have been the final warning sign. Obviously they didn't know a real Canseco from the reproduction. Well I guarantee you today they know the difference. This little episode called "education" cost them 75 big ones.

Q: I see dealers advertising cards for sale at crazy prices. I have seen cards for sale at up to TEN times guide. Are these guys ripoffs or am I missing something?

A: Not all dealers who charge over guide are ripoffs. First of all most guides today on pre-1980 cards list a price for near mint condition cards. So if a card is in near mint to mint condition, or mint condition or gem mint, that means it's worth more, a lot more in some cases, than the price you see in your favorite price guide.

Some of the most classic examples you are probably seeing are cards #1 Andy Pafko and #407 Eddie Mathews from the 1952 Topps set. Here is the case of a common card, that of Andy Pafko and the card of a Hall of Famer, Eddie Mathews. The key here is that both are condition rarities. In other words they are not rare, even though the Mathews card is definitely scarcer than the Pafko card. But both are scarce in mint condition. If mint and centered, then we have a very scarce card that brings way over current price guides. The current Beckett price guide lists card #1 at $1200 in near mint. #407 Mathews lists at $1750. Yet recently both have sold for $20,000 each. The reason is simple. They were mint, they were dead centered. They are rare in this state of preservation. That is why they bring prices many times those listed in the guide.

A few years ago I acquired a mint 1953 Topps card #81, that of Joe Black. I heard that this card was really a scarce issue. Well one way to find out if this was a fact was to put this into one of my phone auctions. Well to say I was astounded by the results would be an understatement. The guide price at the time of the auction was a paltry $5.00. Would you like to guess what the winning bid was? How about 40 times guide value? Yes, the winning bid was $200. Also just in case you thought I had two nut cases who wanted the card, I had over a dozen bidders over the $100 range. It seems this card is one of the five single prints from the '53 set. Back then hardly anyone knew that. Yet anyone trying to complete their set knew that and occasionally you will get some collectors who will pay dearly to get what they need.

Guides are just that, GUIDES. Don't ever forget that!! Guides don't buy or sell cards. They just give the editor's opinion of the card market as he sees it. The guides are supposed to report what's happening in the market place, but sadly too many dealers instead of making their own prices follow what's in their favorite guide. Thus if the guide is off, their prices will be wrong as well.

The bottom line is always with YOU. YOU, the consumer, the purchaser, are the bottom line. A card is only worth what YOU are willing to pay. If a dealer wants $500 for a card and the best offer he can get is $300 he will eventually have to lower his price to that level if he expects to sell it. Otherwise he will be sitting on it and that won't make him any money, and dealers are in business to make a buck.

Conversely, if a dealer has a great card and knows it, he may decide to hang tough and not lower his price and wait for the demand to come up to his asking price. I know this to be the case, as I have had some super choice items which I paid a small fortune for and I wasn't about to sell the item for a loss. I know many of you have been in this dilemma. Sometimes you walk, without purchasing the item. Sometimes you bite the bullet and pay the dealer's price. You hate him, you hate yourself, but usually you end up loving the card and "brag" to your friends what a great card you purchased and what a "super buy" you received based on the card's rarity and incredible condition.

Q: What is your opinion of repaired cards? If the price is right, should I buy some?

A: Most cards which are repaired are repaired to improve their grade and thus technically raise their value. Unfortunately many repairs to a card do NOT raise the value of the card. They actually do the exact opposite. For example, certain type of minor repairs are okay. You can erase a pencil mark off a card. You can remove gum stains from a card. Removing a minor crease is also acceptable. Removing tape from a card is fine as well.

The type of repairs which are not acceptable are ones like the building up of corners to take a card with rounded corners and make it appear to be mint condition. Reglossing a card is not acceptable. Replugging a card with a pinhole and using bleach to whiten a Cracker Jack card are also no-no's.

The repairing of a card is not illegal or immoral. The selling of one isn't illegal either. It's the selling of the card without informing the prospective buyer that the card in question has been "repaired."

Many years ago I sold a 1933 Goudey Babe Ruth card to a dealer for $350. It had some problems with it, so I just wholesaled it to a local dealer. Well several weeks later I saw the card again and couldn't believe it was the same card. It went from very good to near mint to mint condition. This dealer then sold the card to a investor for $3800. Not a bad markup for his time in repairing the card.

This same dealer also told me that half of his income came from repairing cards. He made over $100,000 that year from selling repaired cards. Glad to report he no longer sells cards. But his old customers are not so lucky. They still own many expensive repaired cards which they think are going up in value, but in reality are doing nothing pricewise. Never buy a repaired card if you're purchasing for investment, no matter how attractive the price. I said NEVER!

The Future

Predicting the future, to quote Ernie Pyle, is like "trying to drill a hole in water." It can't be done and shouldn't be done and shouldn't even be attempted, except by fools who have nothing else to do and sufficient money to do it. If you think you can predict the future of the sports-card market you're a fool; even if you turn out to be right you're still a fool, because sooner or later you'll run across a market you can't figure out, and then you'll be in a fine mess. But editors will be editors, and editors want authors of books like these to predict the future, so here goes. If it means I've finally crossed the line into fooldom, so be it. There are plenty of people who will tell you I crossed that line eons ago.

As long as I'm going to be wrong like this, I might as well take a sport-by-sport approach. I'm going to deal in vague generalities because I'd rather be generally wrong than specifically wrong; besides, I've spent the last couple hundred pages being specifically wrong, and I need a break.

THE SHAKEOUT

Whenever someone who's unfamiliar with card collecting and investing encounters someone like myself, about the third or fourth question they ask (after "Is it true Wayne Gretzky paid more than a million dollars for one baseball card?" "How big is the baseball-card market right now?" and "Is it really that big?") is, "When is the shakeout coming?"

People are really, really concerned about the upcoming shakeout in the sports-card market/industry, but the funny thing is, the people outside the market are more concerned about it than the people inside the market. Evidently the people inside the market are either: a) too scared to mention the word, for fear that might trigger the entire collapse; or b) they don't see any shakeout coming.

Well, bless their pointed little heads, because there is a shakeout coming, either a shakeout of collector/investors, a shakeout of dealers, or both. The most likely scenario for a shakeout of collector/investors is this:

All those people who bought, say, 1990 Upper Deck sets as a graduation fund or retirement fund go to cash them in, quite a few of them at once. This sudden influx of several hundred thousand sets on the card market triggers deep price decreases in these cards, which then trigger more selling of associated issues. These price plunges cause even more panic selling—involving small and medium-sized dealers this time—covering more issues, and eventually anything that exists in quantity in high grades is affected. The market for almost all modern material collapses, leaving millions of collectors with billions of cards worth about what they paid for them, or less. They cut their losses and sell for peanuts, pennies on the dollar, leaving the card market devoid of collectors and depressed in value.

There's also the dealer worst-case scenario, which has one or more major dealers—dealers who sell to dealers—trying to get too big too quickly and collapsing, leaving many smaller dealers who placed orders with these bankrupt major dealers without cards and without cash. Since most small dealers rely on one issue to pay off the next issue—they sell football cards to buy baseball, and baseball to buy football, and basketball and hockey to buy whatever—they collapse one by one and start selling off their inventories for pennies on the dollar, causing prices to plunge, leading to panic selling, causing inventories to evaporate in value, causing more small dealers to go under, and so forth and so on, as above.

Either scenario is likely. One actually happened. Big Bob's, one of the hobby's mega-dealers, recently went down, and took as many as fifty small and medium-sized dealers with him. What prevented the market from collapse? Its own momentum. People still wanted to buy cards, and someone had to supply those people with cards. But there's no guarantee that momentum will be there the next time a major dealer goes down—and a major dealer has been going down once every three or four years. In fact, if a dealer goes down at a time when there are no hot issues capturing the buying public's fancy, the whole thing could collapse like . . . well, a cliche: a house of cards.

The tough thing about predicting shakeouts is that they happen more or less independently of other economic events. The recession of 1992 contributed slightly to the near-shakeout that resulted from Big Bob's collapse, but Big Bob's would have collapsed in an election-year economy just as easily. And so many dealers are so undercapitalized it would take just one disruption in the normal chain of events to push them over the brink.

So the answer to the question, "When is the shakeout coming?", is, "Soon." The answer to the question, "How soon?", is either:

a) "None of your business";

b) "Beats me"; or

c) "How soon do you want it to come?",

with the last answer being the most valid. This is an illusory market. People buy cards and make illusory profits on the illusion of scarcity and rarity. They buy into the illusions of limited editions and collectibility. The collectibility of sports cards exists in the heads of the people who collect them. There is nothing inherently collectible or valuable about pictures of sports players mounted on cardboard that exist in the millions. Therefore, there is the danger that at any time any number of the people buying into this notion may realize that the emperor has no clothes, and the whole thing may be brought to a screeching halt. But to paraphrase H.L. Mencken, "No one ever lost money underestimating the ability of the American public, once having fooled themselves, to continue fooling themselves." Don't ask me when the shakeout may occur.

BASEBALL

Of all sports cards, baseball cards have the rosiest future, since baseball cards have been around the longest, have increased in value the most gradually, and stand the greatest chance of retaining some value in the eventuality of a shakeout. There are more collectors of baseball cards than any other sports cards, and more sorts of baseball cards with value. As opposed to basketball cards, where there were only three major sets issued before 1970, baseball cards have many very scarce, very collectible issues from before 1970. These are cards with established values and genuine scarcity, and they ought to withstand anything this side of a nuclear holocaust.

Older baseball cards remain the prime hedge against any collapse in the sports-card market. Many of these cards are actually undervalued compared to modern issues and could conceivably go up in value while the rest of the card market is collapsing. Both sets and singles look good for the long term, with high-grade cards of big-name players, despite their high current cost, having the greatest chance of providing a solid return.

Should an apocalyptic collapse not occur, sets from the '70s and early '80s will outperform the rest of the market, as nostalgia for those days, misguided as it might be, fuels demand and drives up prices. Minor-league cards from this era will also be extremely good gainers, pushed up by the continuing achievements of players like Cal Ripken, Jr., and Rickey Henderson. (The outlook is actually very good for all minor-league cards, as they represent a very mainline sort of contrary investment.) Cards from the '50s and '60s will remain popular and will retain their values well, though as prices continue to increase for these cards grading standards will tighten. It will take a much better Near Mint card to bring a $10,000 Near Mint price as opposed to a $2,500 Near Mint price. Memorabilia will continue to bring record-setting prices, as major auction houses take more and more of this material out of the traditional collector market and put it into the hands of non-hobby investors. Modern rookie cards will soften, as buyer confusion and apathy take the starch out of what had been the market's prime mover.

From the corporate standpoint, the number of card lines will drop by 50 percent within the next three years. Among the casualties: Bowman, Score Pinnacle, Fleer or Fleer Ultra, and Donruss' basic card. Leaf Studio is also on the endangered list. Card lines will settle along three price points, with one or two brands in each. Along with this settling will come a cooling in promotional efforts like holograms, limited-edition inserts and autographed "chase" cards. Profits will be down for all cardmakers, though the profit margins on the manufacture and sale of baseball cards will remain indecently high. Makers of ancillary baseball products— holograms, 3-D cards, silver rounds, statues, autographed plaques —will find their markets no longer exist.

BASKETBALL

Basketball cards have the least optimistic outlook of any of the major-sport cards because of the nature of the game. Basketball is superstar-driven; popularity for basketball cards is directly related to the popularity of its top players. The popularity of Magic Johnson and Larry Bird helped sustain basketball cards through some tough times, and the popularity of Michael Jordan has driven the basketball-card market to new heights.

But if basketball were to lose Michael Jordan and not find a similarly charismatic replacement the market for basketball cards would shrivel dramatically. This is not an idle threat. Basketball sets that lacked this year's top rookies—the new Michael Jordan wanna-bes, as it were—went belly-up. No one wanted first-series NBA Hoops cards or Fleer cards or SkyBox cards, but when Upper Deck came out with its first series, featuring rookies Larry Johnson and Dikembe Mutombo and Billy Owens, people bought.

The impending arrival of Shaquille O'Neal could help the basketball market, but it's an awful lot to ask of him to be the next Michael Jordan. David Robinson, photogenic role model that he is, hasn't quite been able to pull it off. And if Robinson can't, you have to wonder if anybody can.

Even the market for older basketball cards is somewhat predicated on the popularity of current players, and though the current high price levels are likely to be maintained, there may not necessarily be much price movement from those levels. Again, a lot depends on how Michael Jordan finishes off his career; a spectacular denouement could give this market a push it may never relinquish.

Another shadow is being cast on basketball cards by the National Basketball Association itself. The NBA prides itself on control of the game and manufacture of its image, and that extends to basketball cards. The NBA has very distinct notions of what the basketball-card market should be and what issues should fall into what niches. If the NBA, perish the thought, happens to be wrong, if its quest for control of the market goes awry, the whole thing could disintegrate. It's already misread the market once with its SkyBox cards; don't discount the possibility of it shooting itself in the foot again.

There are few income opportunities in basketball cards, no real card history, few sets that are good hedges, precious little excitement, and no guarantee that even this mediocre status quo be maintained. You may be wary of this market if you so desire.

FOOTBALL

What a mess football cards are right now! There are at least twelve cardmakers (Pacific, Score, Fleer, Topps, Pro Set, Upper Deck, Classic, AW, Collectors' Edge, Action Packed, SkyBox, and NFL Properties) and at least twenty sets. No one cardmaker has the permission of both the NFL Players' Association and NFL Properties to use all the players in the league, so every set is a partial set. Collectors are confused and frustrated, and the market is coming off its worst year since the big market expansion of 1989. What a blooming mess it all is.

And the unfortunate thing is that the football-card market is essentially healthy. In 1991 cardmakers sold more football cards than they ever had before, but those sales were spread so thin among so many different companies that it seemed as though the market was in a tailspin. People want to buy football cards and will buy football cards, but for the market to have any sort of long-term capabilities there must first be a shakeout and then a squaring-away—or maybe first a squaring-away and then a shakeout. But somehow football cards have to get their bearings again.

The first and most basic thing that has to happen is for the NFL and the Players' Association to settle their differences. Card sets are being licensed as a means for both organizations to amass licensing money for strike funds. NFL Properties, the marketing arm of the NFL, is signing up players to marketing contracts to weaken the NFLPA's bargaining power. The result is divisive and downright lousy for the football-card collector, who just wants a set of cards with all his favorite players in it. If he doesn't get it, eventually he's going to stop buying football cards, and a good market will go bad. But at least in the short term there will be a measure of forgiveness for football cards.

The football-card shakeout will follow the lines of the baseball-card shakeout but will be more pronounced. Many of the smaller companies that make only football cards or primarily football cards will find the going tough and cease operations. Many of the larger companies that make cards for other major sports in addition to football cards will find fewer hassles and more profits in those other sports and abandon football; these companies could include Score, Fleer and even Upper Deck. The companies left making football cards will be those large companies with football as a base for their operations—Pro Set, basically—and those diversified companies who do well enough in football to justify a continuing presence—Topps, for instance.

The market for older football cards may continue in its current depressed state for a while. While the value levels are high for many older football cards, few cards are trading for those prices. The market for older football cards is full of artificial values, and those values have to either shake out or justify themselves for major action to resume. If prices do fall, the cards will be bargains and should be bought up in quantity immediately as a hedge. There are definite limits to how far the football-card market can fall, and so any decline in prices is likely to be steep and short-lived. Like baseball cards, sets and individual star cards from the '70s and early '80s make some of the best buys, and should outperform the market as a whole over the next five to seven years. '60s cards and sets are at very high levels but are not selling at those levels and should be avoided over the short-term; '50s cards as sets should be viewed as having plateaued.

In general, you'll have to be patient with the football-card market. It hasn't quite got its act together yet.

HOCKEY

Hockey cards are in good shape for the long term because of the faithfulness of hockey-card collectors. The people who have been buying hockey cards over the years are real dyed-in-the-wool collectors; they've been propelling this market, driving up the prices for older cards and keeping them there, for years and years, and there are absolutely no signs of these people abandoning this market. As a result, prices will remain high for older hockey cards and may even go higher. Hockey cards from 1967 and before are among the safest buys in all of cards because there is so much real scarcity of these cards and so much demand for them. Sets and stars from the '70s and '80s will outperform the market slightly over the next several years, with values for Wayne Gretzky cards continuing to rise slightly but cards for other stars—Mario Lemieux, et. al.—gaining ground. The market for newer cards is healthy and will remain so as long as the National Hockey League does not overextend itself granting licenses. There may be some shakeout among manufacturers in terms of the lines and varieties of cards they offer—you probably won't see an American, English-Canadian and French-Canadian version of the same set from the same manufacturer, like 1991–92 Score hockey—but the hockey market appears capable of supporting four or five manufacturers. However, the NHL is acting a little like the NFL and hinting it may fling wide the door as far as licenses go. If it does, there is the potential that this market could become as discombobulated as the football-card market in as little as three years. It's something to watch for.

NON-SPORT

When you ask cardmakers where they feel the future of the business lies, they give you two quick answers: international marketing and non-sport cards. International marketing is crucial because there is, plain and simple, a limit to the amount of cards American consumers will buy, and that limit is being approached daily. With more and more domestic competition squeezing card-makers harder and harder, international markets, with their lack of competition and disposable income to burn, look like the greenest pasture on earth.

The only problem is the fence. Europeans have no card-collecting tradition whatsoever, and have shown no recent inclination to collect cards. As the president of SkyBox International, Frank O'Connell, told me recently, "They know stickers, and stickers are very low-cost products to manufacture and low-cost products to purchase. They're not used to cards where the cardstock costs extra and the photography and printing quality costs extra." Card companies may eventually climb this fence and market their products successfully overseas (the Japanese market for baseball cards being the Holy Grail in this whole undertaking), but for now international marketing makes a better buzzword than it does reality.

For that matter, so do non-sports cards—or entertainment cards, as SkyBox likes to call them. Companies have poured an awful lot of money recently into cards depicting rock stars and Disney characters and Looney Tunes characters and Marvel comic-book superheroes and rap acts and *Guiness Book of World Records* recordholders and scenes from *Star Trek* and *Batman* and *Saturday Night Live,* with definite mixed success. The crossover between comic books and cards seems to be the most lucrative right now for cardmakers; they'll continue to exploit it until it cools. Otherwise, cardmakers are finding that many of these big-money non-sport ventures are handy holes for pouring huge sums of money down. The non-sport market is very fickle, and based on its past history, there's no reason for it to change anytime soon. It could very well resist any attempts to market it into the big time; if it doesn't, there may be some real upward price movement in older non-sport sets. These cards should be evaluated the same way any piece of nostalgia from that particular era is, with little regard for it being a card as opposed to a table game or a raygun. Older non-sport cards should not be the basis of your trading-card investment portfolio, but they do make a nice complement.

OTHER SPORTS CARDS

In the last several years there have been card sets issued for—are you ready?—harness racing, drag racing, Indy-card racing, motocross racing, horse racing, BMX bike racing, stock-car racing, dog-sled racing, track and field, deer hunting, bass fishing, men's bowling, women's bowling, PGA golf, ATP tennis, indoor soccer, outdoor soccer, pro wrestling, skateboarding, international baseball, international basketball, Russian baseball, Russian hockey, boxing, volleyball, table tennis, monster-truck competitions, and jai alai. What do you figure the odds are of any of these surviving and thriving as collectibles are?

Actually, the odds are very good for stock-car-racing cards. Four solid firms—Pro Set, Maxx, Traks and Red Line—make these cards, and sell oodles of them throughout the South and Southeast, wherever the NASCAR circuit runs. Prices for five- and six-year-old cards are substantial, and going up. It's a bit of an esoteric field, so scout it out and learn as much as you can about it before you invest. But the possibility does exist that stock-card racing may join basketball, baseball, football and hockey as one of the major card sports before 1995.

SOME FINAL COMMENTS

This book is meant to be a guide and we hope it's been of some help as such, but you have to realize: This is a screwy market. When you expect it to go right it'll go left, and vice versa. Our expectations are based on the years we've spent in this market, but if every one of our predictions were proven wrong, we wouldn't really be surprised. Manufacturers are learning as they go along; so are buyers and sellers. Mistakes are made right out in the open; everyone can see when you falter. The market is freewheeling and unpredictable. People have called it "the last free market on earth," and I believe they're right. It is free and wild and altogether wonderful, and I can't think of anywhere else I'd rather put my money. I hope you'll come to feel the same way.

OTHER BOOKS FOR COLLECTORS

Collecting Baseball Cards--Third Edition
All-time bestseller
Donn Pearlman
ISBN 0-929387-20-1
123 pages--$7.95 paper

Making Money with Baseball Cards
A handbook of insider strategies
Paul M. Green and Donn Pearlman
ISBN 0-933893-77-9
215 pages--$7.95 paper

The Top 100
The best baseball cards to own, ranked and rated for the investor and collector
Paul M. Green and Kit Kiefer
ISBN 0-933893-88-4
303 pages--$8.95 paper

Collecting Football Cards for Fun and Profit
How to Buy, Store and Trade Them
Chuck Bennett with Don Butler
ISBN 0-929387-32-5
158 pages--$8.95 paper

Collecting Sports Autographs
Fun and profit from this easy-to-learn hobby
Tom Owens
ISBN 0-933893-79-5
131 pages--$6.95 paper